SCOTTISH WOMEN'S STUDIES SERIES

Bajanellas and Semilinas

Aberdeen University and the Education of Women 1860–1920

Lindy Moore

ABERDEEN UNIVERSITY PRESS

First published in the Quincentennial studies in the history of the University of Aberdeen under the same title 1991
This edition published 1991
Aberdeen University Press

British Library Cataloguing in Publication Data

Moore, Lindy
Bajanellas and Semilinas: Aberdeen University and the education of women 1860–1920. — (Scottish women's studies series).
1. Grampian (Scotland). Higher education institutions. Students. Women, history
I. Title II. University of Aberdeen III. Series
376.941235

ISBN 0-08-041202-5

PRINTED IN GREAT BRITAIN
THE UNIVERSITY PRESS
ABERDEEN

Foreword

In 1995 the University of Aberdeen celebrates five hundred years of continuous existence. Some eighty other European universities had been established before 1500, of which about fifty have survived to the later twentieth century, though not all of those with an uninterrupted history. At Aberdeen, King's College and University was founded in 1495, and Marischal College in 1593, the two combining to form a single university in 1860. Such a long institutional life invites close historical study, as well as celebration; but the 1980s were not an easy time for British universities, and it is therefore the more striking that in 1984 the governing body of the University of Aberdeen decided to commission a series of historical studies in honour of the quincentenary. The decision to commit funds to this project, and to give the Editorial Board such a free hand as we have had, makes the University Court's decision the braver and more honourable.

This fourth contribution to the Quincentennial Studies series cross-references with Robert Anderson's *Student Community at Aberdeen 1860–1939*, which was the first in our series to appear. There the social effects of the admission of women to the university were acutely and sympathetically analysed. Here we have a more concentrated study of the debate which preceded women's admission, and a more detailed account of the experience of women students in all its aspects. Bajanellas and semilinas were the year names, adapted from the male equivalents of bajans and semis, which were applied to first and second year women students at Aberdeen University. These names were in part a recognition of the women's status as university students, but they were also half-mocking, and ridicule was one of the strongest weapons employed against women in higher education. As this study shows, the path of women into, and their establishment and progress within the university was not easy. Fortunately there were strong characters among the early women students, and just after the date at which this study ends, one of these women, Mary Esslemont, was elected President of the Students' Representative Council.

There is much of general, as well as of specific Aberdeen interest in this study. It is the more welcome because, though a good deal has been written about the higher education of English women in this period, very little has appeared about their Scottish counterparts.

Lindy Moore is an independent scholar who has for many years made Scottish women of this period her particular object of research. The Editorial Board is pleased that she has devoted her expertise to the benefit of the Quincentennial Studies series, thus illuminating an episode important in the history of this university, but with a wider significance.

JENNIFER CARTER
General Editor

Contents

List of Illustrations

List of Tables and Figures

TABLES

FIGURES

Author's Preface

As Scotland's economic and political independence declined, its educational system was promoted as an example of its cultural and national autonomy. But the tradition of a democratic, co-educational and classless system served to hide both the variations and the inferiority of the educational provision and the educational experience, formal and informal, available for girls and women. Accounts of boys and girls sitting together at the parochial school sharing a common curriculum—a picture in itself open to amendment[1]—were followed by descriptions of the burgh schools, where references to girls tended to become somewhat hazy and confused, and concluded by the triumphal admission of the 'lad of parts' to the university, by which point all references to women had disappeared.[2]

Aberdeen University was founded in 1495, yet women were not admitted as students until 1892. Two questions can be asked: why were women excluded for four hundred years? And what social, cultural, economic or political changes occurred in the late nineteenth century to override such a long-established tradition? This work examines some aspects of the debate surrounding the admission of women to university education in Aberdeen, the reaction to their presence, and the effect of their admission on university culture and on the women students themselves. Several studies have documented the admission of women to universities south of the border; this is the first comparable study of a Scottish university.[3]

I should like to record the debt which I owe to the individuals and institutions who have given me invaluable support and advice over a period of many years. These include the librarians and archivists at the university and public libraries of Edinburgh, Glasgow and St Andrews, the National Library of Scotland and the Scottish Record Office (not least the member of staff who delayed the start of his New Year holiday to allow a researcher to continue to the last possible moment), David Doughan at the Fawcett Library, and especially the staff at Aberdeen

Public Library, Aberdeen University Library and Aberdeen University Department of Special Collections and Archives. Particular thanks are due to Jennifer Beavan, Myrtle Anderson-Smith and Colin McLaren; and to Carla Leslie who gave up holiday time to search out illustrations.

Amongst a number of individuals who kindly attempted to recall bygone days for me, I would especially like to mention Dr Mary Esslemont, Dr Isabella Leitch, Sheriff John Lillie, Mrs Mackenzie Stuart, Mrs Ramsay Ewan and Miss Nan Shepherd.

Thanks are also due to the two people without whom this publication would never have been completed, Donald Withrington and Jennifer Carter. As editor of this volume, Donald Withrington's advice reflected his comprehensive knowledge of the history of Scottish education and his meticulous eye for detail; but perhaps of even greater value was the support and encouragement he voluntarily gave to a novice local history enthusiast many years ago. Independent research by non-academics is not always easy, especially if they are women with young children and I am glad to have this opportunity to record and acknowledge the debt I owe Don. Finally, as series editor, Jennifer Carter has not only given much astute advice, but provided continuous and time-consuming support, both moral and, following my somewhat untimely move to Wales, practical. Any errors of fact or interpretation which still remain are, of course, my own responsibility.

Chapter 1

1860–1883

1860–1877

English reforms in girls' education led to the opening of Queen's College for Women, Bedford College and the North London Collegiate School in 1848, 1849 and 1850 respectively. In 1856 London University refused a petition that women should be admitted to its medical examinations and in 1862 it rejected the admission of women to degrees. The same year the universities of Edinburgh and St Andrews both rejected an application from Elizabeth Garrett who was attempting to qualify as a doctor. However, by paying for private tuition from recognised teachers instead, Miss Garrett gradually obtained all the instruction necessary to meet the qualification for admission to the Society of Apothecaries except for practical anatomy. When she wrote to a number of medical men, offering a fee of £25 for this final course, Alex Harvey, professor of *materia medica* at Aberdeen, gave an unequivocal response:

> fortunately it is not necessary that fair ladies should be brought into contact with such foul scenes—nor would it be for their good any more than for their patients if they could succeed in leaving the many spheres of usefulness which God has pointed out to them in order to force themselves into competition with the lower walks of the medical profession.[1]

Although Elizabeth Garrett obtained a more sympathetic response from John Struthers, then an extra-mural lecturer in Edinburgh but shortly afterwards appointed professor of anatomy in Aberdeen, Struthers indicated the conflicting external pressures and personal doubts that such a request aroused. He had no doubt of Elizabeth Garrett's ability and when she applied to him he felt that, as the only extra-mural lecturer in Edinburgh who could give qualifying classes in anatomy, he could not refuse her. He would not teach her individually, or in a mixed class, but agreed that if other women came forward and formed a ladies' class he would take this, much as he disliked the idea. A class was duly formed, but before the course could begin Struthers encountered objections from his Edinburgh medical colleagues and immediately gave up the scheme.[2]

The proposal that women should be admitted to the universities, which was the subject of a paper at the 1862 meeting of the National Association for the Promotion of Social Science, gained only a passing reference in the Aberdeen press.[3] But despite a similarly negative reaction throughout most of the country, Emily Davies persevered with her scheme to establish a women's college in connection with Cambridge University, while Mary Crudelius founded the organisation which was to have the greatest influence in pioneering higher education for women in Scotland—the Edinburgh Ladies' Educational Association (later the Edinburgh Association for the University Education of Women) in 1867.[4] The aim of this association was to establish an interconnected series of university-standard courses taught by Edinburgh professors, with a university-approved certificate as testimonial: in effect to establish an extra-mural arts faculty for women. But several of the participating professors including the most supportive, Aberdeen graduate David Masson, made it clear that they accepted the scheme only as a second-best substitute for the formal admission of women to the universities.[5] Over the next few years various lecture schemes and university 'higher certificates' for women were introduced by or in connection with the English universities and university colleges and similar if less ambitious schemes started at St Andrews and Glasgow.[6]

Although Aberdeen professors and their assistants had given public lectures to which women were admitted on previous occasions,[7] the changing public perspective was indicated by the fact that when William Milligan, professor of biblical criticism, agreed to give a lecture course for women on the New Testament in 1868, his reference to women's right to pursue whatever academic disciplines took their interest was quoted with approval by the local press and, modest and uncontroversial though the proposed lecture course was, the *Aberdeen Journal* at once connected it with developments in the higher education of women elsewhere and used it as an opportunity to press for the introduction of a more extended and co-ordinated scheme through which Aberdeen professors would provide teaching for women.[8]

The extraordinarily rapid growth of public opinion in support of higher education for women at this date was reflected in the editorial columns of the *Aberdeen Free Press*. In 1868 all female education except that which specifically prepared women to discharge the duties of wife and mother were brushed aside as unimportant. Whilst the domestic emphasis was still retained, the following year it was admitted that more than merely technical training might be necessary to achieve this aim. Fifteen months later the paper was referring to an 'urgent need' for higher education for women and by 1872, not only was the desirability of higher education taken for granted, but the paper was also convinced that this should be achieved by admitting women to the existing universities alongside men.[9]

The most controversial event in Scotland was the attempt by a group of women led by Sophia Jex-Blake to gain admission to Edinburgh University's teaching and degrees in order to become qualified as doctors.[10] Edinburgh University admitted them to separate classes in 1869, but subsequently opposition developed and they were refused further tuition. The women students took legal action against the university but when their success was overturned on an appeal to the Court of Session, they decided not to appeal to the House of Lords, but to concentrate on getting the relevant legislation altered. Unfortunately the largely sympathetic Liberal government was promptly defeated at the general election so, as government action could not now be expected, a private member's bill supported by MPs on both sides of the House was introduced 'to remove doubts as to the powers of the Universities of Scotland to admit women as students and to grant degrees to women'. Although the bill was introduced as a result of the experience of the women medical students at Edinburgh University, it proposed to give each of the four Scottish universities discretionary powers to admit women to any of their faculties.

Of all the interested parties, the position of Aberdeen University was the least easy to determine. None of the university's bodies or committees petitioned parliament about the bill either one way or the other, and no reference to the bill appeared in the minutes of the Senatus Academicus, the University Court or the General Council. In fact Aberdeen kept such a low profile that even those debating the bill in Westminster seemed to be uncertain of the university's stance.[11] In 1874 Sir William Maxwell-Stirling (MP for Perth and rector of Edinburgh University) commented that three of the four universities had, speaking through their constituted authorities, expressed their unwillingness to accept women (the fourth being St Andrews which had petitioned in favour of the bill). The Lord Advocate, Conservative MP for both Glasgow and Aberdeen Universities, also implied that three of the four universities opposed the scheme. He spoke forcefully against the bill, though he was quick to support the principle of higher education for women, on the grounds that the universities would require double the staff and the facilities, an argument which of course assumed that female students would have to be taught separately. But there was sufficient ambiguity about Aberdeen's position for the MP for Marylebone to comment during the 1875 debate that 'Aberdeen and St Andrews might be in favour of the admission of women, Edinburgh and Glasgow might be against it'.

Aberdeen was a conservative university, resistant to change and one which would certainly have wished to avoid finding itself in the contentious position which had afflicted Edinburgh. On the other hand the university was in need of students and was imbued with the tradition of a 'democratic education' based on the old rural parish schools attended by both sexes and all social classes with the university as their goal. As the editorial columns of the *Free Press* had demonstrated,[12] the logical conclusion of this tradition (regardless of whether it was in practice myth or reality) was the free admission of both sexes to the university. Nevertheless, only three of the twenty-two Aberdeen professors were amongst the Scottish professors who signed a petition in support of the admission of women—the independently minded John Struthers; ex-doctor George Dickie, professor of botany; and radical Alexander Bain, influential professor of logic, a local lad of parts and ex-Bedford College lecturer.[13]

The Universities (Scotland) Degrees to Women Bill was finally debated on 3 March 1875 when it was defeated by 194 votes to 151. The three Liberal Aberdeen MPs, J Leith, W D Fordyce and William McCombie, voted in favour of women's admission and Aberdeen Town Council had petitioned in support. Following its defeat the three leading Aberdeen newspapers were agreed that success for the women was merely a question of time; the real source of the universities' opposition lay not in educational grounds, but in the vested interests of the medical profession.[14]

The extent to which formal discussion on the subject had been avoided at Aberdeen University itself became evident when the University Court was presented with an application for recognition by the newly established London School of Medicine for Women; in the course of the debate it transpired that the question of permitting female medical students to come up for examination and graduation had not previously been discussed. Professor Pirie, soon to become principal, aptly typified the institutional attitude—not entirely hostile, yet relieved to discover that positive action could be avoided.[15]

Aberdeen University had one more opportunity to support the idea of formally admitting women to the universities in the 1870s. The Royal Commission on the Scottish Universities was taking evidence, and with this in mind Alexander Bain proposed 'that the Senatus petition Parliament to introduce into any Bill that may be brought in referring to the Scotch Universities, a clause removing the legal restriction to the admission of women'.[16] Struthers, Milligan, John Black, professor of humanity, William Pirrie, professor of surgery and John Forbes, the seventy-five year old professor of Hebrew supported Bain's motion.[17] The recently appointed principal, William Pirie, and Francis Ogston, professor of forensic medicine, abstained. Once again however, more cautious counsel prevailed; an amendment moved by Frederick Fuller, professor of mathematics, that it was 'inexpedient for the Senatus to pronounce on the subject of the admission of women to the Scotch Universities until the subject is brought before them in a definable shape and with a view to a practical solution' was passed, though it was indicative of changed attitudes that the direct negative was not proposed. Those who voted for the amendment included David Thomson, professor of natural philosophy and secretary of the Senatus; James Nicol, professor of natural history; James Brazier, professor of chemistry; William Stephenson, appointed two years earlier as professor of midwifery; and father and son, Samuel and James Trail. Samuel Trail, professor of systematic theology, was an old-fashioned seventy-year old from Orkney. His son later became a committed supporter of the women's cause, but this was the first Senatus meeting he had attended since his appointment as professor of botany and he may have wished to avoid a contentious vote, especially on an issue disapproved of by his father. John Fyfe, professor of moral philosophy, who was known for his idiosyncratic kindnesses to students, later provided an annual prize for the Women's Higher Certificate; and even conservative William Geddes, professor of Greek and, from 1885, university principal, later became more sympathetic to the women's application. At this date, however, Senatus meetings were often the scene of acrimonious debates between 'Bain's party' and the 'Geddes' party', political differences between the chief protagonists being exacerbated by personal feelings. As Professor Hay discovered: 'Scarcely a meeting of the Senate passed without heated discussions interspersed with much of personal jibe and sarcasm—by no means confined to the members of the parties indicated. There were other factors, and other causes for strife.'[18] For the next decade the question of the university instruction and examination of women was to remain one such contentious issue.

The Aberdeen Ladies' Educational Association

Although the adverse judicial ruling in the case of the Edinburgh medical women meant that Aberdeen University could not legally admit women as matriculated students, even had it wished to do so, growing support for higher education for women coincided with proposals from the university's General Council for scientifically orientated extra-mural lectures to be given by the professors.[19] The scientific lecture scheme fell through, but in 1877 a small group of Aberdeen graduates—lawyers and businessmen led by John Duguid Milne—founded the Aberdeen Ladies' Educational Association with the objective of establishing an integrated scheme of professorial lecture courses for women similar to those organised in the other university towns.[20]

The association drew its support from all parts of the political spectrum. For example, Geddes' brother-in-law, John Forbes White, who defeated the 'Bain's' candidate to be elected assessor to the University Court in 1880, was vice-president and both Mrs Bain (an ex-superintendent at Bedford College) and Mrs Geddes were on the executive committee. Initially, none of the university professors had an active role in the new association, though four professors' wives were on the first executive.[21] Indeed, none of the first male directors had any direct educational connections although two, the Reverend Henry Cowan and Sheriff Dove Wilson, were later to become professors at the university. In 1882 the constitution was altered, and those members who had taken no active interest in the association or whose professional activities clashed with the times of meetings, were removed from the executive. At the same time lecturers who had given courses for the association were automatically made directors for the following three years, so that in 1883 five members of the executive committee were Aberdeen University professors.[22]

Each course initially consisted of twenty lectures given over a period of twenty weeks but from 1881–82 the number of lectures per course was doubled. (This compared with 100 lectures for undergraduate courses.) Although the Aberdeen association preferred professors to take the course, unlike the Edinburgh association, it did not insist on this, aware no doubt that such a precondition would have been untenable at the smaller institution.

The annual reports on the progress of the classes at first emphasised that the progress made proved that it was possible for women to undertake more advanced study. Later, as standards developed and staff and students became more confident, more specific comparisons were made between the women students and the university undergraduates. In 1882 Bain's successor, William Minto, reported that the women had been given the same English lectures and examinations as the male undergraduates; that the first-placed woman had tied with the first-placed university class prizewinner; and that altogether six of the thirteen women who had taken the examinations would have gained class prizes.[23] Minto recommended that the women's success should be reported to the local press for publication on the same day as the list of university prizemen. Otherwise the lecturers' comments did not vary much over the seven years; polite reference was always made to the courtesy, interest and intelligence displayed by the students, to the exceptional zeal of a few and the hard work of all. Attendance rates were high, often despite bad weather, and most of the lecturers obviously enjoyed teaching their classes.

1 John Duguid Milne of Ardmiddle and Melgum (1822–89).
From George Washington Wilson, Aberdeen portraits, group no. 3, no. 66.

Unlike previous occasional lectures or lecture courses given by Aberdeen professors for interest and entertainment, the intention was to supply a comprehensive and co-ordinated educational course at secondary/higher level to supplement the education of middle-class girls who had just left school; the women students were therefore urged to work hard and to study at least two subjects simultaneously.[24] But the handful of upper or upper middle-class Aberdeen women who wanted advanced education went south to the more comprehensive courses being provided at Oxford, Cambridge, London or Edinburgh. Other middle-class parents who might have permitted or even encouraged their sons to attend university could be expected to refuse permission for their daughters to attend classes which might actually lessen their marriage prospects. There were few potential governesses in Aberdeen; most middle-class girls who had to work came from poorer rural professional or lower middle-class families and looked to school teaching as a career, and such girls could not afford the time or the money for expensive courses which provided no recognised qualification or certificated training. Nor could the lecture hours be arranged so as to be convenient for working teachers as well as for the professors who had other classes already timetabled, and for the social visiting conventions of middle-class leisured women. Consequently most of the students were married women attending the classes out of interest, rather than recent school leavers using them as the basis for a course of further education, and only a quarter of those attending studied at least two subjects at a time.[25] The later classes lost their less dedicated members because of the more demanding nature of their syllabuses after they were reorganised to help those who wished to study for Aberdeen University's Higher Certificate for Women introduced in 1882, but the reorganisation did not produce the hoped for increase in higher certificate women, because most of these preferred to work instead for the St Andrews' LLA, which could be studied at home with the help of correspondence courses and offered a title on completion. After six years the number of women attending the association's courses dropped. In 1883 the classes were cancelled, and in 1886 the association was formally wound up and the residue of its funds given to the university's Local Examinations Board to be awarded as prizes.

One problem had been that the association had been unable to raise sufficient funds or to attract any endowments, and so lacked the financial resources which would have enabled it to guarantee the core subjects independently of student numbers.[26] A second difficulty had been the amount of effort that had to be put into the courses by the lecturers. Professor Struthers commented that although he had 'never taught a class with more genuine pleasure, from day to day, nothing would

2 John Struthers, professor of anatomy, 1963–89. *AM* 8 (1888–89), facing p 87.

induce me, with all my desire to promote the higher education of women, again to undertake such a course in the midst of my university teaching.'[27]

Within a few years of its inception, association members had no longer questioned whether any of the women in north-east Scotland could reach the standards of the male university students; the women were passing the Aberdeen and St Andrews' higher certificate examinations in growing numbers. In 1882 Milne argued that the association was simply 'the fortunate instrument of inaugurating a new relation between the university on the one hand and an interesting section of the youth of this country on the other' and that the closer and more direct the connection was between the two the better it would be for both. If the university took direct charge of the association's classes it would mean very little more work than many of the professors were already engaged in on the association's behalf, but the classes would be much more influential and acceptable to the public and would have a prestige, an educational importance and a stability which the classes of a voluntary organisation could never hope to achieve.[28]

The collapse of the Aberdeen Ladies' Educational Association led an increasing number of those who supported women's higher education to the view that the only practical and equitable means by which women could receive education of university standard was by their admission to the universities; either on the same terms as men, or to a separate institution specifically established as a university for women, which might be completely independent or linked to an existing university through a collegiate system. The collegiate system was not traditional in Scotland, but colleges existed at St Andrews, while Queen Margaret College, taught by Glasgow professors, but registered as a limited liability company, provided an example for women. An independent college would solve the difficulties surrounding mixed classes and recalcitrant professors, and could be supported by those who favoured a different higher education curriculum for women.[29] But such a development was opposed for precisely these reasons by those who wished women to have identical opportunities to those of men, and by those who believed in the democratic tradition in Scottish education because, they argued, Scottish women would only be able to support one such institution and the lack of local university provision for women would be unjust as it would place poorer women at a disadvantage.[30]

The 1883 Universities (Scotland) Bill, which made provision for the creation of University Commissioners to investigate and recommend the reorganisation of the Scottish universities, made no substantive provision for women, although some thought that the discretionary powers which the Commissioners were to be given were wide enough for them to introduce an ordinance on the subject. The Ladies' Educational Association executive was more cautious:

> Your Directors, however, judged it very unsafe to rely in a matter so important, upon the doubtful interpretation of a general clause; and at a full meeting of the Directors, specially called for the purpose, your office-bearers were empowered to prepare a Memorial to Her Majesty's Ministers, and Petition to both Houses of Parliament, praying that in the Bill there should be introduced instructions and powers to the proposed Commission to make provision for the Higher Education of Women at or in connection with the several Universities of Scotland.[31]

This memorial thus left open the options of admitting women to the universities on the same conditions as men, or of introducing some arrangement whereby the universities took control over the existing associations and their extra-mural classes and established women's colleges.

Chapter 2

Certificates and Titles

The Aberdeen University Local Examinations

In 1864 Edinburgh University followed the example of Oxford and Cambridge and instituted its own scheme of local examinations. Like Cambridge it admitted girls to the examinations, although as Cambridge did not formally admit girls on a permanent footing until 1867, Edinburgh could be said to have been the first university to admit girls on equal terms. It seems to have done so rather by default however, as the issue of female candidates was not specifically discussed. Similarly, whenever the question of establishing similar examinations was raised at Aberdeen in the 1860s, it was presented simply as a scheme for testing the education of boys[1] and since the bursary competition was often taken as a trial of standard by boys who had no intention of entering the university, there was felt to be no need for a second examination.

The Edinburgh Locals were poorly supported until the mid-1870s when the Edinburgh Ladies' Educational Association began promoting the examinations as a positive means of improving the education and schooling of middle-class girls in Scotland. This influenced the newly formed Aberdeen association, which adopted a similar policy and several of the association's members, including Professors Milligan and Struthers, publicised the Edinburgh Locals.[2] The Aberdeen association was at first hesitant as to whether it should press for Aberdeen to establish its own scheme, but subsequently it was decided that this would be preferable, largely because of the perceived danger of local schools and teachers losing their individuality through subjection to the control of a remote board of examiners.[3] Meanwhile, the Aberdeen School Board had sent in its own request that the university should institute local examinations for the benefit of pupils leaving the Aberdeen Grammar School or other town schools without the intention of taking a university course. The implication that boys as well as girls might be interested in the scheme, and the plea that the unique standards of the North East were at stake were strong arguments. The fact that Glasgow University had by then introduced its own local examinations scheme and St Andrews had re-introduced its scheme, leaving Aberdeen the only Scottish university without such examinations, no doubt also influenced the decision and Aberdeen's first local examinations were held in 1880.

Later there were criticisms that Aberdeen had dragged its feet on the issue of helping the education of local girls:

> Where our university is open to the reproach of lagging behind is in its failing to start these examinations for years after they had been successfully held by all the other universities of Scotland; when it was well understood that these examinations were, in the meantime at least, mainly for women, and although we were specially urged to do so with the view of doing for the education of the women of this district what the other universities had done for the women of their districts.[4]

Figures for candidates by sex were only provided for the first year. On that occasion girls constituted 80 per cent of the Preliminary candidates, 72 per cent of the Ordinary/Junior candidates and 100 per cent of the Senior candidates. Comparative figures for passes were available by sex each year. In the first year boys did very much better than girls in the Ordinary Certificate, but less well in the Preliminary Certificate. No boys took the Senior Certificate that year and only a handful ever went on to do so. Over thirty-one years a total of 4,972 girls and 330 boys passed the Preliminary Certificate examination; 2,160 girls and 191 boys passed the Junior Certificate examination and 3,300 girls and twenty-one boys passed the Senior Certificate examination.

Members of the Local Examinations Board frequently expressed regret at the imbalance of male and female candidates. John Struthers recommended that boys intending to enter the university as medical students should sit the local examination instead of the medical preliminary examination which was of a very low standard,[5] but his suggestion was not taken up and the Locals ran the risk of becoming second-class examinations for girls only. John Black supported them, but still considered the more exclusive university bursary competition (from which girls were excluded) the better test.[6] In the event, however, it was to be the Leaving Certificate introduced by the Scotch Education Department in 1888 which fulfilled the function Black and Struthers had envisaged.

The Local Examinations did not become an important part of Aberdeen University's development. Though the university retained its scheme longer than any of the other Scottish universities, its size and influence was paltry when compared with the Cambridge or Oxford examinations or even with those of Edinburgh or Glasgow. Nevertheless, the scheme provided the important first step of formal responsibility by the university for the education of female pupils, and a useful means of raising the standard of some of the more progressive of the local private girls' schools.

Aberdeen University Higher Certificate for Women

One of the main aims of the Aberdeen Ladies' Educational Association had been to obtain university recognition for, or examination of, its courses. Milne had included the subject in the draft memorial he had prepared in 1878 but informal inquiries of the professors and others interested in the association led the committee to report that the general view was 'that we are not yet ready for it, however much we ought to keep it before us as a thing to be aimed at'.[7] The question remained in abeyance for two years until Milne made the more definite proposal that the association should ask the university to institute a higher university examination for women in connection with the association's classes, to be rewarded with a diploma on the lines of the university certificate being offered by Edinburgh and Glasgow Universities. The association's committee members were still hesitant[8] but agreed that they should at least advise the university of their aspirations, and now that a suitable extra-mural examination infrastructure had been established and experience gained with the Locals, the professors proved more enthusiastic. Accordingly, Milne's memorandum was officially presented to Senatus which referred it to the Local Examinations Board; this reported in favour of the certificate and the first examinations for the Aberdeen University Higher Certificate for Women were held in 1882.[9]

In theory the Higher Certificate, although administered at Aberdeen by the Local Examinations Board, differed from the Local Examinations because it was open to women only and was supposed to be of university MA standard. A third distinguishing feature, attendance at the association's classes, was not made compulsory, so the certificate became simply an external examination similar to the St Andrews LLA, rather than dependent on professorial tuition as in the case of the Edinburgh certificate. The most contentious aspect of the Aberdeen Higher Certificate was the university's decision not to award a diploma in connection with the examination. The association submitted a memorandum regretting this decision and emphasising the difference between the local examinations which aimed simply at directing and systematising existing secondary education and the contemplated higher examination for women which would need to induce women to undertake advanced study.[10]

The assocation was justifiably anxious about the competition resulting from the recently introduced St Andrews diploma of Lady Literate in Arts (LLA), already establishing itself far more rapidly than the certificate courses offered to women by Edinburgh and Glasgow Universities. In 1883 there were 64 successful candidates at the LLA centre opened that year in Aberdeen, compared with five candidates for the Aberdeen Higher Certificate. Girls were entering for the LLA from those private schools in the city which provided most of the Aberdeen Senior Certificate pupils and even from some of the burgh and elementary public schools[11] which had traditionally looked to the local university where the education of boys was concerned. Between 1886 and 1896, 525 girls who sat the St Andrews LLA had previously taken the Aberdeen Local Examinations and so might have been expected to move on to the Aberdeen Higher Certificate.[12] The figures for the Aberdeen Higher Certificate for Women were feeble by comparison, never reaching twenty a year and the association's fear that 'the direction of this branch of higher education in our district will fall into extraneous hands' was realised. There were financial considerations too; in 1885 the total income from the previous year's LLA examination was £816 whilst by that date the Aberdeen Higher Certificate had produced an annual revenue, since its inception, of £6![13] When George Pirie, professor of mathematics, betrayed his frustration by questioning the motives of local girls who chose the LLA, Gustav Hein, later a lecturer at the university, argued that women students intending to be teachers needed a title to compete for jobs in England.[14]

Senatus responded positively to the association's memorandum, appointing a committee to inquire into the legal powers of the university to institute new degrees and to ascertain the views of Edinburgh and Glasgow Universities on the propriety of instituting such a diploma.[15] The committee, however, was advised that there was no great point in altering existing procedures because of the probability of a University Commission being appointed in the near future which would reorganise the entire structure of the Scottish universities.[16] But governments move slowly, and it proved to be another seven years before the Commission in question was appointed; in the meantime the initiative to establish a women's diploma at Aberdeen was choked.

Most of the professors were convinced that the success of the LLA was due to the title St Andrews awarded,[17] although after the failure of the Aberdeen lecture scheme John Struthers was more sceptical about the assumption that a title would greatly increase the popularity of the Aberdeen certificate.[18] It was also argued that a title such as that offered by St Andrews was illegal, although that consideration had not stopped St Andrews, nor prevented Aberdeen University itself from instituting the Local Examinations. William Milligan and William Minto were amongst those who supported the idea of some kind of title for the Higher Certificate.[19] Struthers, who firmly believed that teaching should incorporate practical and demonstration work rather than rely on theory, was characteristically outspoken in his opposition; no one had done more than himself to promote the higher education of women, he remarked, but he did not approve of the St Andrews' LLA: 'That piece of tinsel, that piece of gewgaw' was destroying the reputation of the Scottish universities. He recommended that the Scottish universities should instead combine to provide a respectable qualification for women.[20] Charles Niven, the young professor of natural philosophy, praised St Andrews for taking the lead in Scotland in the provision of higher education for women, but he too was critical of its solution, preferring the direct admission of women to the universities. James Trail argued that a title or diploma for women was only a half measure and should be rejected in favour of admitting women to the university, claiming this would be a much less radical alteration to its constitution than converting it into a non-teaching examining body with a concomitant lowering of status.[21]

In 1886 Alex Mackie, the influential head of Albyn Place, a private girls' school, presented a paper on university higher certificates for women at a meeting of the Aberdeen branch of the Educational Institute of Scotland.[22] He supported the admission of women as university students but, given the proverbial slowness of university and state machinery, considered the objection to temporary half measures was ridiculous. He advocated the introduction of a title for the Aberdeen University Higher Certificate, believing it would result in many north-east girls choosing the Aberdeen examination, especially since he also considered, having taught both, that the Aberdeen certificate was the better examination. He thought that the LLA placed too much emphasis on memory and set too many prescribed books, with the result that the questions tended to be very superficial. He was also critical of the tendency to include works expressing opposing views, arguing that students at this stage were too immature to cope with this without supporting literature. He preferred the Aberdeen syllabuses which were less 'showy' but hung together better.

Mackie thought the objections raised by the Aberdeen professors to the institution of a title were largely based on pique at St Andrews' breach of university etiquette in stealing its rivals' students with its 'glittering bait'. He agreed that a title would probably be illegal, but pointed out that such a consideration had not deterred other university initiatives. So far as the objection to a non-teaching university was concerned, Mackie argued that the professors did not provide all the teaching for the existing arts curriculum; university assistants also lectured and extra-mural mathematics coaching was provided for many students.[23]

3 Alex Mackie and Albyn Place School's Higher Certificate for Women class, 1897, G I Duthie and H M E Duncan, *Albyn School Centenary 1967* (Aberdeen, 1967), p 22.

Despite Mackie's support for the Aberdeen Higher Certificate there were no candidates at all in 1887, and the professors appealed for suggestions as to how to increase the examination's popularity. Mackie and two other Aberdeen teachers who were preparing candidates for the LLA presented a memorial recommending the introduction of a title, the grouping of subjects, an increase in the minimum number of subjects needed for a pass from three to five, the introduction of lower fees than the LLA and a restriction in the number of subjects that could be taken in any one year to three.[24] Minto suggested that the Local Examinations Board should ascertain local feeling on the subject. This was agreed, along with Struthers' suggestion that the committee should also consult with the Senatus of Edinburgh and of Glasgow Universities.[25]

Accordingly, twenty-five circulars were issued to various teachers and to the secretaries of Local Examination centres in the North East requesting their views. Of the fifteen replies, thirteen were in favour of the university granting a title for the Higher Certificate, while the other two considered that the university should undertake full responsibility for the teaching of women. Minto promptly proposed:

> That in view of the strong local feeling that a title should be conferred on successful candidates for the Higher Certificate, the Board recommend that a title be conferred; the subjects for that Certificate to be revised; suggest that the title should be L.L.A. or A.L.I.; suggest further that, except in Modern Languages, none but pupils of University Graduates presenting themselves at Local Examination Centres within the Aberdeen University area, i.e. north of Brechin, be eligible for the title, and that part of the Examination be oral and conducted in Aberdeen.[26]

Struthers objected that the board had not yet received any information about the views of Edinburgh or Glasgow Universities and therefore should hold back its report to the Senatus. His motion was carried and the subject was not raised again by the Local Examinations Board.

Despite the failure to grant a title, the number of candidates reached double figures for the first time in 1889, and averaged thirteen per year over the next decade, confounding expectations that the opening of the university to women from 1892 would result in the decline of the Higher Certificate. The weakness of the Higher Certificate was the narrow base of its support; there were never more than five schools in any one year presenting candidates and on several occasions only one school did so, despite continued attempts to increase the certificate's popularity—in 1897 the regulations were altered after consultation with the schools involved and the fee was reduced to half a guinea. Nine per cent of the successful candidates came from state aided elementary schools and eight per cent through private tuition, but increasingly the continued existence of both the Local Examinations and the Higher Certificate was becoming nothing more than a university favour for the handful of local private schools which provided 80 per cent of the entrants.

Most candidates for the Higher Certificate chose English, social science and modern language subjects; planning the syllabuses in these subjects must have provided the university staff with valuable experience when the subject choice of the arts degree was widened following the 1889 University Commission. Almost all the girls took English and French. Before 1894 logic and psychology, history and German were the most popular third choices. After that period the number choosing logic declined and history became the third choice of most candidates. From 1903 onwards mathematics was sometimes selected by Albyn Place or St Margaret's pupils and one girl achieved 100 per cent. Given that the standard of the Higher Certificate was even roughly comparable with the MA degree it was remarkable that any schools were able to present candidates for this or the LLA examination and it illustrated the general improvement in the standard of education offered to girls at many of the public and private schools in the North East during the last quarter of the nineteenth century.

So far as Aberdeen University was concerned, however, the story of the Higher Certificate was one of growing anxiety amongst the professors and those who supported their *alma mater* as they saw their potential clientele slipping away from the university at the same time as the admission of women to the universities became increasingly likely. In 1890 over 600 girls passed the LLA while only five passed the Aberdeen Higher Certificate. Despite their desire to increase student numbers, however, the Aberdeen professors felt even more constrained by the views of their more influential colleagues in Edinburgh and Glasgow, who were themselves based in sufficiently cosmopolitan and populous centres to attract women students without instituting a title.

Chapter 3

Debate on the Admission of Women to the University

Arguments presented against the higher education of women have been examined by Joan Burstyn, who found that the concept of 'womanliness' was an important means of social control in Victorian society, because it permitted women to be treated as an entity rather than as individuals. Admission to higher education countered this by enabling women to achieve intellectual status and possibly occupational status through their own efforts rather than having them ascribed by reference to their male relatives. It therefore gave women the opportunity of moving into men's sphere and out of their own parallel but relatively powerless domestic sphere.[1] Burstyn identified three types of argument used by those who opposed women's admission to higher education; economic arguments against the movement of women into middle-class occupations, arguments based on contemporary social conventions and biblical authority and arguments using evidence from comparative anatomy and physiology.

In a long article published in the *Free Press* and reprinted in a revised version as *The Admission of Women to the Scottish Universities*, Christina Struthers summarised the main objections to the admission of women which had been raised in Aberdeen:

> that women were never contemplated in the establishment of our Universities, which have been organised and equipped exclusively for men; that to admit women would be contrary to the intentions of those who founded them; opposed to the wishes and injurious to the interests of those at present in possession of these institutions; mischievous to the public interest; and lastly bad and undesirable for the women themselves.[2]

Occupations

The admission of women to higher education was seen as a preparatory step to enabling them to enter professional occupations, a point tacitly admitted by many women's supporters, but resulting in strong opposition from the professions and many male students.[3] In the 1840s, however, J Duguid Milne had proposed to the Aberdeen intelligentsia that middle- class women should be encouraged to take up paid employment, and he had published on the subject in 1857.[4] Milne had advocated the development on moral and cultural grounds which reflected the influence of Enlightenment ideas, but for many North East families there were more practical reasons. Few were really wealthy or could expect a pension for the main income earner and many women, even some professors' daughters, had to be prepared to find employment.[5] Though domestic duties, including aid to less fortunate relatives, were expected to have priority, self-dependence and a useful employment of time were seen as activities to be encouraged by middle-class presbyterians, and proposals to expand employment opportunities for women and encourage their take-up received increasing support from the more serious and liberal of the local periodicals. At the least, it was argued, artificial restrictions should be removed, leaving it to experience to show whether women were fitted for professional employment or not.[6]

The professions most immediately affected by the issue of university education for women were medicine and teaching. The idea of medical women provoked the more hostile reactions, but might also be supported by those who felt most strongly on the issue of separate spheres and differing moralities for the sexes, since they most disliked the idea of women being medically examined by men. Though conservative attitudes and medical trade unionism were apparent in Aberdeen,[7] there was also town and university support for women who wished to receive a medical training.[8]

The position of female teachers was frequently cited as a reason for approving the admission of women to the Scottish universities. In 1873 the Church of Scotland had been permitted to open a teacher training college in Aberdeen, provided that it admitted only women, and the following year the Free Church followed suit. At the same time trainee teachers who were Queen's Scholars were permitted to attend some university classes for the first time. Initially this arrangement did not apply at Aberdeen because only women students were permitted to enter the training colleges there and only male training college students were permitted to attend the universities, but it meant that after 1873 women teachers who wished to be admitted to the universities had a case to argue based on practical rather than abstract justice, and the foundation of chairs of Education at Edinburgh and St Andrews in 1876 further strengthened their case.

The educational tradition of the North East, with its high proportion of graduate teachers in the parish schools, had special consequences for female teachers. On the one hand female teachers were seen as automatically inferior and subordinate to male teachers;[9] on the other, it was felt that if women were to be admitted into the local public schools at all, they should receive a university education in the local tradition, a view which could be held by those who believed in women's intellectual and professional inferiority[10] as well as by those who did not. 'Nothing could be more unfair and absurd than that schoolmasters should have the benefits of a university training, while schoolmistresses are absolutely shut out from any such advantages' argued the editor of the *Aberdeen Free Press*.[11] Belief in the importance of women teachers influenced the attitude of the influential ex-schools inspector, Professor Black; initially opposed to mixed classes for pupils over the age of fourteen or sixteen, by 1876 Black was advocating the admission of women to the Scottish universities so that they would be competent to teach secondary subjects.[12] As a result of special encouragement under the presidency of William Rattray, the Aberdeen branch of the Educational Institute of Scotland had the largest number of female members of any branch in 1878, and supported university training for women teachers in 1883. Aberdeen school board teacher, Isabella Chalmers, gave papers on the subject in 1881 and 1883; Christina Struthers used the issue as a central part of her argument for the admission of women, and the rector of Robert Gordon's College was another local educationalist who referred to the likelihood of both men and women teachers receiving university training in the future.[13]

In 1884 Aberdeen University applied to the Scotch Education Department for permission to establish a system for training teachers. Although the printed correspondence does not suggest that the university had given any thought to the possibility of including women, Craik later described the Aberdeen proposal as encompassing both men and women students, the suggestion being that the university should receive £100 for every male teacher and £70 for every female teacher who, having gone through their classes, went on to obtain a teaching certificate.[14] But the SED was opposed and the Universities of Glasgow and Edinburgh, who could afford to be fussy, objected to proposals to involve the Scottish universities with teacher training on the grounds that it would lower university standards; in 1886 Aberdeen University was bought off by being allowed a few male training college students.

Whilst female teachers could not be formally admitted to university classes, some informal attempts were made to provide for their special needs, their lower incomes and their restricted free hours. The Local Examinations fee was reduced for pupil teachers, for example, and when the Aberdeen Ladies' Educational Association raised its lecture fees the lower rate was retained for teachers. In 1877 John Struthers obtained permission from Senatus to hold a class on the structure of the human body for intending teachers. That the demand was there was evident from the fact that in 1882, when he arranged to hold his Ladies' Educational Association lectures on a Saturday so that teachers could attend, they constituted almost half of the students.[15]

Social conventions and religious beliefs

Women were the main recipients of home, church and school teaching on the appropriate subservient and domestic role of women. It was, therefore, not surprising that they often held stronger views on the subject than their male colleagues, for they had been more thoroughly socialised. As women were usually expected to take responsibility for their daughters' education, such views were self-perpetuating. Professor Milligan, for example, arranged for his eldest daughter to be sent to the new girls' school, St Leonards, at St Andrews, but his wife objected to Louisa Lumsden's advanced views and recalled her daughter on the pretext that her help was needed with the younger children.[16] The Aberdeen Ladies' Educational Association was another example. It was formed as a result of the efforts of local men rather than women, and the minutes show that the female members were often conservative and hesitant about pressing their claims and that Milne, more radical and more self-confident, frequently tried to persuade them to adopt a more positive approach. In 1879 a member of the association who reported that there had not been as yet 'any intention on the part of the Aberdeen University authorities of conceding to women university education in any complete or extended sense' had also to admit that there was in fact:

> no strong or general feeling in Aberdeen as to its necessity. The Ladies Association resulted mainly from the efforts of an earnest minority and has not been supported hitherto with very marked enthusiasm by that section of the community on whom its development must ultimately depend.[17]

There were no major public attacks on admitting women to university by Aberdeen professors or other local figures; no conservative champion spoke out in public as Sir Robert Christisson did at Edinburgh. Women's threat to the existing system was much less strong in Aberdeen and conservatives were by definition reticent about making public comments about woman's role and nature unless the matter was seen as urgent. Conventional ideas and behaviour were reinforced by the use of sarcasm and innuendo, both in personal relationships and in local periodicals such as *Bon Accord*, a light-hearted illustrated satirical magazine, which

4 William Milligan, professor of biblical criticism 1860–90.
AM, 7 (1889–90), facing p 173.

reinforced the conservative views held by many, probably the majority, of the non-intellectual middle class. *Bon Accord* contained many references to those examinations which were taken chiefly by girls or women, the Locals, the training college examinations and the LLA, implying that the use of sex appeal would enable female candidates to obtain passes from the male examiners and containing references to the unacademic approach to study adopted by girls, with the implication that if this was not the case it should be, because neither logic, competitiveness nor sustained concentration were characteristics consistent with femininity or 'womanliness'.[18]

The contradiction between 'womanliness' and higher education was expressed even more clearly in *The Castle Sceptre*, a private magazine largely written by teenage girls. The father who acted as editor set the tone when he criticised the proposals to establish a ladies' educational association or to encourage girls to enter the Local Examinations; knowledge would degrade women and (crucially) it would destroy marriage because women would no longer submit to their husbands, right or wrong.[19] Again, sarcasm was a frequent weapon. According to one extract the students at Girton College consisted of those who had lost hope of being women, wives or mothers and so were trying to 'make men and bores of themselves'.[20] When the Reverend Iverach, an Aberdeen minister who was later principal of the Aberdeen Free Church College, objected to half the population being denied a university education, a *Castle Sceptre* contributor went on to prove that truly feminine women could not benefit from an intellectual education despite their best intentions and therefore those who did benefit were not properly feminine (domestic and God-fearing) women:

> All women who have to work for their daily bread . . . say we give them too much education. No women who marry have time for university education. Most other women do not want such education. Mr I's 'one half' is thus reduced to a few thousands, and these not the most estimable of their sex. Does Mr I. know that some of the most fascinating of our agnostic writers are learned ladies . . . Why are women, however much they may learn, unable to come to the knowledge of the truth? Because they are women, and therefore their nature is emotional, not intellectual; because they are not subjected to that rude contact with the world which eliminates much of the speculations of the mere closet student, much of what is sentimental, fanciful, and unsound.[21]

If a private publication of this sort indicted the attitudes common amongst many of the middle-class families in Aberdeen, one of the girls brave enough to attend the LLA classes at the High School described from personal experience the 'many objections and sneers' that the female pupils faced. On the one hand the girls were accused of being learned; on the other, of simply liking to have initials after their name. And of course they were inevitably asked what use the qualification would be later; whether it would help in the keeping of a house or the cooking of dinner.[22]

Similar criticisms expressed by the university students in their debates and newspapers were made with all the egocentric confidence natural to those convinced of their own inherent superiority and importance: women's role was considered simply as one of providing for men's emotional and material needs. It was argued that the higher education of women would result in the sacrifice of the emotional to the intellectual, while the superior knowledge women would acquire would be of no use for domestic affairs and would make them less attractive companions. And not only would it be incompatible with their performance of their home duties, but it might also encourage them to move into public and professional activities, with disastrous consequences for family life.[23] A student who criticised a vote of the University Debating Society against admitting women to higher education argued that women shared common human characteristics with men and that in their capacity both as humans and as mothers, it was better if women were well educated. Men specialised in the professions; women should develop their artistic side so as to make their own lives and the lives of those around them more bright and beautiful. He added that they should also familiarise themselves with science because nothing was more irritating than the habits of inexact thought prevalent amongst young women.[24] Another student objected that a leisurely study of the fine arts, higher literature, music and a little science (a syllabus for women with which he broadly agreed) did not constitute higher education.[25] That implied the study of certain specific subjects (particularly classics and mathematics), studied to a set standard within a fixed time and tested by examination. Women should never study under pressure, he asserted, but he recommended that between the age of seventeen and twenty they should study a modern language and some English literature, read (but not write) poetry and learn to paint, play tennis and music. They would then be suitably prepared for marriage. This writer did not believe that a training in higher education was the best means of achieving the end in view—making women better wives and more interesting companions. He argued that there was a 'psychical distinction' between the sexes. This was the result of nurture and would disappear if women received the same mental training as men. Up to 'a certain point' education made the mind supple and elastic; beyond that it would become muscular and sinewy and this 'strong-mindedness' would be as objectionable in a woman as would the physical development with which it was being compared. Men desired 'intelligent women with large hearts, not intellectual women with large heads' and the one could only be developed at the expense of the other.

Those who supported women's higher education often sympathised with the view of women as relative beings and tried to meet the criticisms on the opposition's terms. An Aberdeen High School pupil argued that there was no reason why a sound intellectual education should hinder a woman's housekeeping ability; indeed it should be a positive advantage. Nor should any worthy man be afraid of a well-educated woman; her home would be the more refined and she would be able to 'ennoble and elevate' all those with whom she came into contact.[26] This frequently cited argument implied a special 'feminine' morality and overlapped with the conservative view that woman's social influence resulted from her domestic, relational role. Ten years later the male students agreed that women should be sufficiently educated to fill any position in which they might find themselves but that, above all, a good education was necessary because of the considerable influence women had over men in their capacity as wives and mothers.[27]

One way of trying to limit the moral damage once it was evident that women were inevitably being drawn towards opportunities for higher education was through the institution of organisations which would try to ensure that such education retained a solid religious base, thus preventing the development of that agnosticism and lack of understanding about the moral importance of woman's 'proper sphere' which opponents feared. In 1888 a Perth delegate to the Women's Conference on Women's Work described the objectives and organisation of the Christian Woman's Educational Union to an Aberdeen audience.[28] She argued that it was the duty of Christian women to cultivate their natural abilities and that it was 'a great mistake—one might say a sin—if they allow higher education and accomplishments to be cultivated only by those who do not care for religion'; but in the same address she warned that it was 'equally important to lead all girls to carry on their studies in a Christian spirit . . . by regularly using the Bible for practical as well as intellectual purposes' if religious doubts were to be avoided.

Other supporters adopted a feminist stance, originating either from liberal 'rights of the individual' doctrines or from religious views on the value of the individual soul. In 1886 one student 'made the sensible remark that women were the best judges of the matter, and that it was a piece of impudence for the students to settle it one way or the other'.[29] Support also came from the university principal, Pirie:

> It has been put on the footing of their delicacy that they should not be allowed to attend these classes with young men and especially some of them [i.e. medical classes]. My own opinion is that ladies must have their delicacy

> left in their own keeping—it won't do for us to make them delicate. If a woman thinks, as my belief is, that she may attend these classes without her delicacy being in any degree tainted, let her attend them by all means.[30]

This approach was adopted by Christina Struthers who invoked a 'higher authority' to support her argument that women 'must be left, as our catechism says, to the freedom of their own will'.[31] She argued that abstract justice over-rode all objections. Women should have a chance of the best possible education and the opportunity to decide for themselves whether a university course would be undesirable.

Burstyn suggests that the right of women to a liberal education 'for the sake of their development as individuals' gained little support at this time. 'Middle class society did not favour learning for its own sake, nor did it yet define the rights of the individual in terms of equal opportunity to education.'[32] In Aberdeen, however, the positive value of education in itself was frequently mentioned, whilst the concept of 'justice' or 'fairness' pervaded local attitudes,[33] leading in some cases to support for issues such as higher education, medical training or political suffrage for women by those holding otherwise conservative views. Milligan, for example, supported Bain's motion to admit women to the university from a belief in justice and the right of the individual to self development, despite his grave misgivings about the physical ability of women to cope with the rigours of student life.[34]

Professors were very much part of the local and national, social and cultural milieu in which such views, both for and against higher education for women, were being expressed, and their own comments on the subject reflected this. Although it is likely that they were more readily influenced than non-academics by a presumption of the inherent value of higher education, this meant that they were also more inclined to believe that such education had the potential to revolutionise relations between the sexes.

Principal Pirie considered the suggestion that some men were jealous of women being highly educated so strange that he investigated it. He found that 'there were a few of the male sex who had adopted this opposition, but they are very few'.[35] Milligan, a respected minister and influential educationalist, ascribed the 'dewomanising' criticism to men who were afraid that their own inferiority would be revealed when compared with well-educated women.[36] Nor did he see any reason why higher education should make women impatient with the housewifely duties which none but they could fulfil. Deeply committed to improving female education, Milligan had a class-oriented perception of the required reforms. He concentrated most of his energies on improving the domestic conditions of the working classes by campaigning for more and better domestic training for elementary schoolgirls; but so far as upper middle class women were concerned, he argued that technological advances had resulted in an easing of domestic chores and left them with time on their hands.[37] It was true that women had previously managed without higher education, but contemporary intellectual developments meant that women must be highly educated if they were to be able to understand and influence the thoughts and aims of men.

Milligan did not consider that extra-mural classes could ever be an adequate alternative for women because he believed that much of the benefit of a university education derived from its atmosphere rather than from the actual teaching; nor was he alone in believing that quite apart from the question of fairness or savings of economy or labour, co-education would be positively beneficial for women at university level.[38] Like Christina Struthers, Milligan also thought the presence of female students would lead to a much needed improvement in the behaviour of the male undergraduates. On the danger of 'associations' being formed outside the classrooms, a very real anxiety amongst the parents of some of the male students, Mrs Struthers pointed out that the kind of women who attended the universities were likely to be far more respectable than those whom young and lonely male students might otherwise meet.[39] Brother and sister could share lodgings and studies, the sister thus performing the dual womanly functions of providing for her brother's comfort and by her presence saving him 'from many a risk and sore temptation'. Thus it was implied that women could combine academic study with domestic duties and a 'feminine' morality which would have a beneficial influence on the corporate spirit of the university.

Biological and intellectual factors

Although Milligan supported the Senatus motion for the removal of the legal restriction against the admission of women in 1876, he argued the following year that university education was unsuitable for women because they would enter into the spirit of competition and in their eagerness to do well 'they would simply be killed off'.[40] Nor was he alone in this concern. Women may not have been as delicately nerved or highly strung in comparison with male students as Milligan suggested, but the high death rate among male students and young graduates was a striking feature of university life in nineteenth-century Aberdeen,[41] and women suffered additional physical disadvantages as a result of tight lacing and social attitudes which discouraged exercise or healthy eating. The question of women's physical ability to survive higher education without damage to their mental or physical health was frequently raised in the national press and became so contentious an issue that in 1890 Mrs Sidgwick published a report comparing the health of Oxbridge women with their non-student sisters.[42]

At first the Aberdeen women's supporters remained cautious—either because they were more conservative than their counterparts elsewhere, or perhaps to pre-empt criticism and reassure anxious parents. When the Ladies' Association courses were increased from twenty to forty lectures, the choice of subjects was deliberately reduced so that no student should attempt more than four classes a week. 'It is hoped that this arrangement may sufficiently meet the demands of the students without overtasking them.' Similarly, the memorial from local teachers asking the Aberdeen Senatus to raise the standard of the Higher Certificate suggested that a limit should be placed on the number of subjects that might be taken in one year.[43] In 1883 Williams, English master at the girls' high school, wrote of his anxiety that girls would be overworked while preparing for the Local Examinations; even a reasonable amount of mental work required muscular exercise to relieve the brain, he argued, but girls did not get as much exercise as boys, and as they were not as strong as boys mental work took more out of them.[44] He did not subscribe to the 'fixed energy' theory, however, and unlike its Cambridge protagonists considered more exercise rather than less mental effort as the appropriate solution.

Even though girls had only recently started participating in a system of external public examinations there was a tradition in Scotland of their public participation in school examinations, and it was not surprising that although they were aware of the controversy, the Aberdeen professors were satisfied that girls were not being harmed by their academic study for the university's examinations.[45] Struthers, pointing to the hard physical labour done by working-class women, blamed much of middle-class women's weakness, both physical and mental, on lack of appropriate exercise.[46] Stephenson, professor of midwifery, placed little emphasis on sex in a paper analysing the health of Aberdeen children for an EIS congress, except to mention that boys were under a longer period of developmental strain than girls.[47] John Harrower, professor of Greek, forthrightly blamed the spasmodic outburst about examinations on 'outside agitators' who did not appreciate the need for educational incentive and seemed to assume the professors were unaware of the failings of the system.[48] However, Geddes, his father-in-law, did believe that the undergraduate syllabus led to many of the university students being overworked, a situation he considered was being exacerbated by increasing competition and by such factors as the alteration in the age qualifications for the Indian Civil Service.

Fortunately, despite Geddes's gloomy prognostications, the students' mortality rate had declined by the 1890s when the question of women's admission to the university finally became a serious proposition, and in the meantime Scottish women had proved they were both mentally and physically as capable of tackling courses of higher education as men. As early as 1883 Milne, who had previously suggested that most women should sit the Higher Certificate and that only the exceptional should attempt a university education, had become confident that women of 'ordinary talent' could achieve degree standard as readily as men.[49] As the responses of the male students showed, belief in women's different and weaker intellectual abilities was widespread,[50] but the Ladies' Educational Association courses and the Higher Certificate examinations had given many of the professors personal experience of women students' capabilities and without necessarily settling the argument, had proved their ability to reach university standards, even though these had risen considerably during this period. The liberal Milligan and the conservative Geddes both went further and publicly stated their belief that men and women were of equal, if not necessarily similar, intellectual ability.[51]

Institutional and educational considerations

The 1883 Universities (Scotland) Bill, which contained no specific reference to the question of female students, was withdrawn in the face of criticism over its financial provisions. A new bill introduced the following year, which was equally silent on the question of admitting women, again faced considerable criticism from individuals and bodies at each of the four universities, although almost all favoured, or at least anticipated, some reform, and wanted an end to the state of uncertainty which had existed since the 1876 Universities Commission. Bills introduced in 1885 and 1886 were also unsuccessful, though they were significant for women because they did include a clause specifically giving the Commissioners who would be appointed under the act the power to consider the position of the universities with respect to women. The bill presented in 1887 was, in contrast, much worse because it omitted this clause, and it was harder for women to argue that the Commissioners' general powers included the power to admit women to the universities once two previous drafts had implied that such powers required a specific clause. The *Aberdeen Free Press* commented:

> One remarkable instruction given to the Commissioners in the last Bill has now been dropped, namely that which empowered them to make ordinances enabling the Universities to admit women to graduation, and to provide for the necessary instructions being given to them by professors. No

> such clause appears in the present Bill, though it is possible that the larger general powers conferred on the Commissioners may cover this concession to the rights of women. Perhaps it was found that the last Bill was cutting a little before the wind, that Scotland was in no hurry to admit women to its universities. St. Andrews and Aberdeen have different tales to tell on this subject. The ladies may be left to let their desires be known. Considering the failure of the 'higher certificate' at Aberdeen, we can hardly say that there is a burning zeal for university education among the female portion of our university constituency.[52]

The sour attitude of the *Free Press* reflected the paper's dislike of local women attaching themselves to other universities; but lack of demand by women themselves was an argument frequently used by opponents of the women's movement as a reason for refusing to grant women new concessions such as medical training or suffrage, as well as university education. Critics could thus argue that they were doing precisely what the supporters of the women's movement wished, namely letting women themselves decide on the changes they wanted. As with most debating points, the argument could be applied by both sides. Professor Niven suggested that the success of the LLA demonstrated that a striking demand for higher education existed amongst Scottish women, the number presenting themselves for examination in 1888 (237) being almost equal to the total number of male students presenting themselves for degrees at all four Scottish universities thirty years earlier.[53]

Despite the reservations of some individuals, the final draft of the Universities (Scotland) Bill, which became law in 1889, did contain a clause giving the Commissioners appointed the power to permit any of the universities to admit women to graduation and/or to the universities' teaching faculties. It was however to be some time before the Commissioners were able to consider the subject at length and it was not until 1892 that the ordinance relating to women received the Royal Assent and could be applied. In the interval the subject hung in suspense, although the act that the ultra-conservative Professor Harrower referred to historical precedents and contemporary developments respecting the university education of women in his 1889 introductory address to undergraduates showed the extent to which the outcome was, by then, taken for granted.[54] Yet although the admission of women to the Scottish universities was a development in sympathy with the general mood of the times,[55] there were still difficulties and objections and the shape of the final outcome was not necessarily evident at this point. Most of the English and Welsh universities and university colleges established in the late 1870s and 1880s had made some provision for women, but of the older establishments only the non-residential University of London had admitted women to degrees.[56] The collapse of the Aberdeen Ladies'

Educational Association in 1883 meant there was no local pressure group and the secretary of the Edinburgh Association for the University Education of Women anxiously begged Aberdonians to give active support to the relevant clause and not permit it to become a dead letter.[57]

The ordinance which was finally issued was enabling, not compulsory, and despite the opposition of those who felt that the universities should teach all whom they examined, the ordinance made specific provision for the extra-mural education of women if required. Each of the universities thus had to decide, firstly, whether it would admit women to graduation and if so in which faculties; secondly, whether it would provide teaching facilities for them and if so in which faculties; and, thirdly, if the university was to provide teaching for women, whether this should be provided by opening the existing classes or by establishing separate classes for women. Furthermore, since all professors appointed before the ordinance took effect had the right to refuse to teach women, the outcome could be affected by the decisions of individuals as well as the constituent bodies of the universities. The interaction of practical considerations, personal inclinations and previous institutional developments meant that although all four Scottish universities took advantage of the ordinance, their arrangements differed.

The questions raised on the subject in Aberdeen by three of the women's older supporters, William Minto, John Struthers and William Milligan, indicated the variety of issues which were seen as either affecting or being affected by the admission of women to the university. Although Minto was critical of the university's lack of action about admitting women to examinations, he was ambivalent on the matter of instruction.[58] Both the liberal/utilitarian debate about the purpose of a university education, and the question of the place of classics in the curriculum, had been ongoing issues for much of the century;[59] Minto felt that a reorganisation of the curriculum was greatly needed and feared that if women were admitted immediately the defects of the existing system might be perpetuated, whereas a reorganisation was likely to be influenced by the knowledge that women would be participating in the new curriculum. He complained that in some respects men's education was worse than women's, and argued that the university should learn from girls' schools the importance of modern languages and literature.[60] His views reflected those of Alex Mackie, who had argued a few years earlier that even if women were given permission to attend university classes straight away, they would be neither able nor (if they had any sense) desirous of doing so:

> The arts curriculum is not in the line of girls' schools and even if the schools were to alter their plans for the sake of bringing their pupils into consonance

5 William Minto, professor of English, 1880–93. *AM*, 6 (1888–9), facing p 129.

> with the University classes, they would be conferring a doubtful benefit on their scholars. If women are to attain degrees only by passing through the fire to the Moloch of Classics, I for one think they will be wise to remain without a degree.[61]

Minto favoured a university degree for women because it would ensure a permanence in the higher education of women that had previously been lacking and he wanted the university to confirm degrees on women regardless of whether it was decided to arrange classes for them, although he admitted that the distinction between graduation and instruction was new to Scottish universities. But he did not share Struthers' or Mackie's criticisms of the LLA and was quite happy for the university to grant degrees to those taught outside the university, so long as they were well certificated.

However Minto considered the practical difficulties raised by the lack of accommodation in the lecture rooms were greater than Christina Struthers had implied;[62] sufficiently great, indeed, when combined with the university's shortage of funds, to explain why the University Court had not taken any action regarding the admission of women by the autumn of 1890. Lack of finance had been a matter of such concern to the university that four years earlier a memorial had been submitted pleading that, as a result of increasing student numbers and new teaching methods, the need for new accommodation was so great that it was threatening to interfere with the efficiency of the university; the possibility of yet further demands being engendered by the admission of female students had not then even been considered.[63]

Struthers had become less happy as the years passed about the means by which women were to obtain university education. In 1883 he had advocated simply that parliament should compel the universities to admit women to graduation and to bursaries: 'If Parliament would do that professors would soon find a way of providing education for women.'[64] But he had become increasingly doubtful about introducing mixed classes, especially in medicine, and in 1890 (retired after 26 years as professor) he expressed concern that the subject had not been adequately discussed by the university. He was strongly opposed to any attempt to separate the teaching and examining functions of the university, and was afraid that if women who had not been taught at the university were admitted to graduation this would prove the thin edge of the wedge, but his experience with the Ladies' Educational Association had left him convinced that professors could not teach double classes.[65]

Milligan welcomed the admission of women but he believed that the majority of women, possibly even the majority of those who wished to attend university, would be unable to do so; and he envisaged the Higher

Certificate continuing, or in the case of Aberdeen developing, into an alternative form of higher education for many Scottish women. He regarded the obstacles facing women as first, the priority which had to be given to household duties and secondly, parental opposition. Considering only the case of upper middle-class women who did not need to become wage-earners, Milligan believed many parents would hesitate about permitting their daughters to undertake the required study because of the discipline necessary and the concomitant change in their daughter's role from 'fireside ornament' to student with inky fingers poring over books late at night. He was also still concerned about women's health and although he no longer worried, as he had fifteen years earlier, that ordinarily healthy women would be unable to cope with undergraduate courses, he emphasised that it was parents' duty to ensure that their daughters had the physical strength to complete a university course.[66]

Chapter 4

Admission to University Instruction and Graduation

In the summer of 1890 Aberdeen University's General Council held a special meeting to propose the admission of women for graduation and instruction. Only one graduate present opposed the motion.[1] Meanwhile Professor James Trail summarised his views on the admission of women for the University Commissioners who were preparing the ordinances:

> The means of instruction and the Degrees granted by the Scottish Universities should be extended on the same terms to women.
>
> Where the nature of the subject taught is such as to render it undesirable to have male and female students present together provision should be made for their instruction separately; but in all other subjects mixed classes should be permitted, if not, indeed, enjoined. Women have already proved their fitness to pursue the studies taught in Universities; and are entitled to equal justice with men as regards access to such studies and to the Degrees that reward proficiency in them. Justice is not done by giving women merely a Diploma without free access to classes, or access to classes while refusing the Degrees and the rights of graduates. Experience has not shown objectionable results from mixed classes so far as I have been able to learn from personal observation in different countries and from the information given me by the teachers in such classes.[2]

In February 1892 the Aberdeen Senatus reported that it had no comment to make about the draft of the ordinance which would permit the admission of women to graduation and/or teaching in the arts and medical faculties of each of the Scottish universities.[3] Aberdeen was, in fact, the only one of the four universities not to propose some alteration or raise some objection about the proposed ordinance, a state of affairs which may perhaps have given Trail's personal communication greater weight. The ordinance was, however, also carefully considered by the new Students' Representative Council which, taking its responsibilities very seriously, had formed a committee to consider the draft ordinances as they were issued and was the only SRC to comment on this one. With a kindly feeling for the difficulties that might be encountered by fellow-students, the SRC objected to the part of the ordinance which permitted women to receive recognised extra-mural instruction (if none was being provided by the university) 'within the University Town, or within a reasonable distance thereof' and requested that the geographical restriction should be removed.[4] Unfortunately the Commissioners responded by deleting only the last part of the phrase, with the result that the geographical location was even more restricted in the final ordinance.

Several months then passed without the Senatus Academicus or the University Court taking any positive action about admitting women. Eventually P J Anderson, the rector's assessor on Court, heard that the University Courts of both Edinburgh and St Andrews had passed resolutions admitting women and that in each case the University Court had acted on the initiative of the Senatus. Since no similar move had occurred in Aberdeen, Anderson took matters into his own hands and gave notice that he would introduce a motion on the subject before the University Court.[5] The students, hearing of the forthcoming motion, formally proposed:

> that the Student's Representative Council of Aberdeen University, understanding that the Lord Rector's Assessor has given notice of a motion . . . desires to place on record its satisfaction that the claim of women to receive a full academic training has been recognised by the University Commission and its respectful hope that the University Court of the University of Aberdeen will see fit to open freely of the doors of that university without respect of sex.[6]

The students concluded by giving themselves a metaphorical pat on the back: 'This resolution is memorable in as much as the Council in none of the other Universities have up to this time taken such a step. Who shall say that Aberdeen students are behind the age?'[7] The actual motivation behind the motion seem to have been more prosaic, the proposer arguing that such a major change to student life could not pass without some response from the students and if they were not actually to oppose it they must therefore support it!

Anderson achieved his object of getting Senatus to take up the initiative, the professor of forensic medicine, Matthew Hay, giving notice of a motion proposing the admission of women. Senatus agreed that the various faculties and the science committee should consider the question and present their reports at the July meeting[8] and anticipated the decision by also recommending to the Court that 'provision be made at both colleges for proper accommodation for students in regard to waiting rooms, committee rooms etc. and such conditions as to accommodate severally students of both sexes'. Two weeks later Hay moved that the favourable faculty reports should be approved and that a representation on the admission of women to graduation and instruction should be made to the University Court. Pirie reserved his opinion on the report of the medical faculty which had recommended the admission of women to medical degrees, but was the only faculty to decide 'meanwhile' to make no arrangements for teaching women.[9]

At the University Court held on 12 July 1892, it was formally resolved 'that under Ordinance no. 18 General no. 9, Section 1, this Court sanction the admission of women to graduation in all Faculties of the University of Aberdeen'. The only dissenting voice came from Major Ramsay of Barra who objected to the word 'all'.[10] The draft ordinance had provided only for the admission of women to the faculties of arts and medicine, although the Commissioners had indicated that the question of their admission to science and music faculties might be considered at a later date. Sir William Thomson had attempted to persuade his fellow Commissioners to alter the wording to enable the universities to admit women to any faculties they wished, but was defeated by one vote in favour of a version which empowered the universities to admit women to arts, medicine, science and music only. Thomson had demanded his dissent be minuted, on the grounds that the Commissioners' powers under the act in respect to this matter were purely permissive. Criticism from various quarters, including the General Council of Edinburgh University and the Edinburgh Women's Liberal Association, resulted in the final ordinance being widened in the manner Thomson had proposed.[11] It was ironic that Aberdeen, which alone had made no objection to the restriction of the original draft (or had not appreciated its significance), was the only Scottish university which immediately admitted women to graduation in all of its faculties.

Anderson had originally intended to propose that the university should admit women to instruction as well as graduation in all subjects, but he modified his motion to bring it into line with the Senatus recommendations, appreciating that 'it might be inadvisable in present circumstances to offer instruction to women in every subject. This would be most acutely felt in medicine, where alone there would be valid arguments against mixed classes.' Accordingly he proposed that the University Court should request the Senatus to report on the specific arrangements that should be made for the teaching of women.[12] The professors reported that there would be no special problems about admitting women to the existing classes in arts, divinity or science. The faculty of law gave a similar report, but decided that the class of medical jurisprudence should be treated in the same manner as the medical classes. Only Robert Reid, professor of anatomy, objected to teaching women in his ordinary class, but he offered to give a separate class of practical anatomy under his own supervision. This meant that the professors did not intend to delegate any of the teaching of women to extra-mural lecturers and therefore did not have to take advantage of the options in the ordinance which specifically enabled them to do so. Senatus accordingly recommended the admission of women for teaching to all faculties except medicine where a decision was deferred until women students should actually apply.[13]

When one woman applied for admission to the medical course in 1895, the medical faculty duly reconsidered the matter and Senatus passed on its recommendation:

> that arrangements should be made provisionally within the University for the instruction of women in all subjects qualifying for graduation in medicine . . . It was further recommended that it be left to the discretion of the individual Professors in the medical faculty, either to admit the women students to the ordinary classes or to institute separate classes for their instruction.[14]

The relatively unproblematic experience of admitting women to the arts classes and the large drop in the number of male medical students (numbers had fallen by almost a quarter in the three years since the question of providing medical teaching for women had last been discussed) no doubt influenced the decision. The professors concerned decided that teaching would be in mixed classes except for a few subjects such as forensic surgery, midwifery and practical anatomy, but the arrangements for separate teaching do not always seem to have been carried out. Professor Low, who was the demonstrator in anatomy that year, recalled that the single woman was taught alongside the men in those classes too. 'But she was a sensible woman and a very good student. In hospital work she may have met with a little of the traditional obstruction—not all the doctors would have her at the bedside.'[15] No official mention of the attitude of the Aberdeen hospital authorities occurs though presumably they were consulted. Yet obtaining permission for women to be admitted to hospital wards for clinical work had been (and in some cases remained) one of the most contentious aspects of the medical training of women.[16]

The somewhat casual attitude to the arrangements evident at Aberdeen seems to have continued. In 1909 Matthew Hay informed the Committee on Scottish Universities that there were one or two medical classes 'where there must be a certain amount of division and a certain amount of extra instruction'; and in reply to a query about laboratory work he replied that he thought the women students worked alongside the men in the science laboratories and for physiology too, though 'in Anatomy a certain amount of separate provision is made, or used to be made for them, and to a slight extent in one or two other departments', a sufficiently vague response to indicate that the matter was not a burning issue.[17]

Aberdeen was one of only a few universities to admit women to instruction in mixed classes in its medical faculty in the 1890s. Though labour saving for the lecturers, the arrangements did have some disadvantages for the women. Because only odd lectures were involved, the medical professors would occasionally request women students not to attend a forthcoming class without providing any alternative instruction. In the inter-war years women were still not allowed to attend the lectures on rape or shown how to use a male catheter in the clinical sessions, which resulted in at least one qualified woman doctor having to ask her male colleagues for assistance.[18] Nevertheless, in the long term, Aberdeen's arrangements proved to be more satisfactory for the women students and cheaper for the university than those of Edinburgh and Glasgow. In 1909 the Aberdeen University representatives were alone in reporting that the university did not require any special financial assistance to provide for female students as such in any of the faculties.[19]

The ordinances passed by the University Commissioners introduced changes in the regulations controlling admission to the universities. In 1892 the preliminary examination was made compulsory and all students had to study for at least three years after passing this entrance examination before graduating, though private (non-matriculating, non-graduating) students were still admitted. A joint board of examiners was established to bring the four universities into line, and the system of providing junior classes—of secondary school level—at the university was first restricted, and then abolished.

These changes led to a decline in the number of students in the arts faculties in all the Scottish universities, but especially so at Aberdeen. It was suggested that this was due, firstly, to the change in subjects from the old bursary competition to the new entrance examination; secondly, to the fact that the country schools on which Aberdeen University largely depended were unable to adapt to the new curriculum and circumstances as rapidly as the larger and better equipped town schools; and, thirdly, as the Ladies' Educational Association had foreseen, because the attendance of women students had not developed as fast in Aberdeen as at the other Scottish universities.[20]

Eleven women attended undergraduate lectures in October 1892 as private students, most of them attending only Professor Minto's course of lectures on English literature. None of them had taken the preliminary examinations nor was aiming at graduation, although most of them had previously sat the university's Senior or Higher Certificate. The following year six women began following a complete course for one or two sessions,[21] but it was not until 1894 that the first twenty matriculated female students entered the university.

6 Isabella Asher (Mrs Caesar), first matriculated women student. *AM*, 12 (1894–5), facing p 35.

As table 1 shows, in 1895 Aberdeen had the smallest number and the lowest percentage of female students in Scotland. Edinburgh and Glasgow Universities were benefiting both from their proximity to more populated areas and from the prior existence of comprehensive courses of higher education for women which had been run in parallel with the official activities of the universities and were of a standard to permit some women to be awarded degrees retrospectively. St Andrews, with neither of these advantages, had the largest proportion of female students as a result of its well publicised support for women students and its established connections with many schools through the LLA diploma. Aberdeen compared poorly, because it had to start from scratch in its efforts to provide facilities and attract female students. Initially too, many of the North East women registering as medical students preferred to go to Edinburgh or Glasgow where there were well-established separate training facilities for women,[22] while the university's one radical move, the admission of women to the faculties of law and divinity, did not meet a felt need and was not taken advantage of.

TABLE 1 COMPARATIVE NUMBERS OF MATRICULATED SCOTTISH WOMEN STUDENTS 1895–6

	Arts	*Medicine*	*Science*	*Music*	*Total Women*	*Total All Students*	*% Women*
ABERDEEN	34	1	—	—	35	782	(4.5)
ST ANDREWS	37	—	—	—	37	212	(17.5)
EDINBURGH	160	*	2	5	167	1835	(9.1)
GLASGOW	167	72	3	—	242	2825	(8.6)

(* Women attending the Edinburgh medical schools for women were not included in the returns.)

The proportion of female students subsequently increased faster at Aberdeen that at the other Scottish universities. By 1907–8 the number of women students at Aberdeen had risen to 256, forming 31 per cent of the student total, compared with 40 per cent at St Andrews, 24 per cent at Glasgow and 18 per cent at Edinburgh. Thereafter the rate of increase levelled off at each of the universities and the same proportional intake was evident at the outbreak of war, the 337 female students at Aberdeen constituting 32 per cent of the total in 1913.

Medicine and arts were the two largest Aberdeen faculties throughout the period 1890–1920. The remaining three faculties together accounted for about one hundred students (men and women) in the 1890s and 200 by

1913–14. Few women took anything other than arts; by 1899 a quarter of the arts students were women and by 1913 they formed almost half the faculty. This was understandable, for whilst many of the men were intending to make their subsequent careers either in the church or in the legal, medical or scientific professions, there were few employment opportunities for women outside teaching. Education had been accepted as a university subject and intending teachers were now permitted to attend the university arts curriculum as Queen's/King's Students under a local committee (without being connected to a training college) and then take a six-month postgraduate course in education.[23] Other women were attached to the teacher training colleges and attended the university to take only one or two specialist subjects, usually English, a modern language or education. Ironically, in view of earlier anxieties about women students' health, the heaviest workload was carried by students at the teacher training colleges or under the Provincial Committee which replaced the denominational colleges, who attended concurrent courses. These students, most of whom were women, attended a full course at the university with the intention of graduating at the same time as they attempted to obtain the General Certificate and qualify as elementary teachers. In 1908–9, indeed, 71 men and 116 women (almost half of the female arts students) were attempting the double course.[24]

There were always a few female students amongst the two or three hundred men in the medical faculty, though the number actually declined prior to the First World War. In 1913, however, numbers almost doubled to reach thirty and during the war the number increased rapidly, due in part to a deliberate university policy of recruiting at the local schools for potential female medics,[25] so that by the end of the war there were 124 female medical students altogether. Although women took science subjects as part of their arts course, they were slow to enter the new science faculty. For several years only one or two women took the BSc degree, and not until 1907 did their numbers reach double figures. However, since the total number of science students was small, by 1913 the thirty-one female science students constituted a quarter of the total faculty. No women studied law until 1918.

The number of women in the university was greatly increased by the presence of non-matriculating student teachers who attended non-graduating classes, generally taught by non-professorial staff. In 1898–9 twenty-five students were attending special classes for teachers in modern languages. The number jumped to 189 in 1900 and increased steadily thereafter until by 1907–8, after the formation of the Aberdeen Provincial Committee for the Training of Teachers which organised a full non-graduating course, initially provided by the university, there were 311 such students, all but twenty of whom were women (compared with a total of 256 matriculated women students) attending classes in eighteen different subjects.[26] Almost the only complaints came from medical professors who grumbled that the Medical School 'was in danger of being ruined through the flooding of the University quadrangle with girl students', and from the matriculated female students who complained that the student-teachers were taking their seats in King's Chapel.[27]

Arts students took seven subjects for their ordinary degree or five subjects for an honours degree (altered to five and three respectively in 1908). There was some difference, but also much similarity, in the selection of subjects by male and female arts students.

TABLE 2 RANKING OF SUBJECT CHOICES OF GRADUATES, 1901, 1911, 1921.[28]

Subject	*Men* 1901	1911	1921	*Subject*	*Women* 1901	1911	1921
Science	1	1	1	Mod. Lang.	1	2	2
Classics	2	2	3	Science	6	1	1
Philosophy	3	3	2	Philosophy	3	3	4
English	4	4	4	Classics	2	4	5
Mathematics	5	5	7	English	4	5	3
Education	6	7	9	Mathematics	5	6	6
Pol. Econ.	—	8	6	History	8	7	7
Mod. Lang.	7	9	8	Education	7	8	8
History	8	6	10	Pol. Econ. / Celtic / Geography	—	—	9
Law	—	10	5				
Comp. Psychol.	—	11	12				
Eccles. Hist.	—	—	11				
Celtic	—	—	12				

The women's choice of subjects varied more from year to year than that of the male students, though by 1921 the latter were taking a greater variety of subjects. The introduction of tighter regulations in 1914, making one language, one philosophy and one science subject compulsory, made little difference to the overall pattern. In 1901, the women's selection was similar to that of the men, except that modern languages rather than science were the most popular option. Over 90 per cent of the 1901 women graduates chose French as an option and almost half selected German. Though the percentages dropped to 57 per cent and 21 per cent respectively for 1921 graduates, this division of study remained very popular and was only overtaken in the ranking by science because this consisted of five options (natural philosophy (physics), chemistry, botany, zoology and geology) whereas only two

7 Johanna Forbes, Latin assistant. *AM*, 21 (1903–34), p 17.

modern languages were offered. Before the war natural philosophy was the most popular of the science subjects with both male and female arts students, but thereafter zoology became more popular. Latin declined in popularity as a graduating subject more quickly for women than men: 90 per cent of the 1901 women graduates took Latin as a graduating class (a higher proportion than the men), but by 1921 only a quarter of the women were doing so and the re-introduction of compulsory Latin in 1928 affected women more severely. Only a handful of women ever took Greek to this level, but a larger proportion of women than men took mathematics in 1900, 1910 and 1920, though the percentage declined for both sexes.

The honours degree was a new creation; most students, male and female, took the broad ordinary degree. In 1898 there were 389 matriculated arts students, of whom twenty-six graduated that year with honours, including the first two women. By 1901, twenty-one women had received degrees, twenty MAs and one MB ChB. The overall proportion of male and female students taking honours between 1901 and 1925 was almost equal; women constituted 47 per cent of the total number of arts students over this period and 42 per cent of those taking honours; 14 per cent of the medical students and 12 per cent of those taking medicine with honours.[29] By comparison, 34 per cent of men, but only 16 per cent of the women studying for the science degree took honours over the same period. The number of women graduating with honours in any one year was sufficiently small for a few outstanding students to affect the ratio but overall the proportion of women graduating with honours in arts was roughly constant during this period, though women formed a far higher proportion of the MA honours graduates in the first decade of the twentieth century than in later years.[30]

In 1899 and 1900 women graduated with first class honours and received university prizes for English and they continued to do especially well in English, education and Latin. In 1901 a woman won the Dr Black Latin prize and the Seafield Latin prize and was *proxime accessit* for the Town Council Gold Medal awarded to the most outstanding arts graduate of the year. In 1900, 1901 and 1902, women won prizes for anatomy, and in 1904 the Ferguson Scholarship (open to all four Scottish universities) for mental philosophy.

It was creditable for the early women students to do even moderately well in view of the relative educational deficiencies they had faced, especially in some of the most traditional university subjects. Many students could not afford to stay on for the fourth year[31] and although the cost may have been equal for both sexes, the North East probably reflected the general tendency for greater expense to be laid out on sons (from whom greater returns were expected) than daughters. The

TABLE 3 DEGREES AWARDED BY ABERDEEN UNIVERSITY 1901–25[32]

	Numbers		*Percentages*	
	Men	*Women*	*Men*	*Women*
MA	1107	1089	31.1	62.5
MA Hons	468	334	13.1	19.2
(Total MA)	(1575)	(1423)	(44.2)	(81.7)
BSc	175	96	4.9	5.5
BSc Hons	90	18	2.5	1.0
BSc (Agriculture)	182	1	5.1	0.1
BSc (Forestry)	17	—	0.5	—
(Total BSc)	(464)	(115)	(13.0)	(6.6)
BD	89	—	2.5	—
BD Hons	17	—	0.5	—
BL	36	—	1.0	—
BL Hons	21	1	0.6	0.1
LLB	40	—	1.1	–
LLB Hons	13	4	0.4	0.2
(Total law)	(110)	(5)	(3.1)	(0.3)
MB CM	14	—	0.4	—
MB ChB	1131	185	31.8	10.6
MB ChB Hons	106	14	3.0	0.8
(Total medical)	(1251)	(199)	(35.2)	(11.4)
EdB	3	—	0.1	—
BCom	56	1	1.6	0.1
Total	3565	1743	100.2	100.1

	Ordinary	*Honours*	*Higher*	*Honorary*
Men	2850	715	347	406
Women	1372 (32.5%)	371 (34.2%)	8 (2.3%)	1 (0.3%)

Carnegie Trustees believed that the increase in the number of students taking honours was in part due to the financial support they provided from 1901.[33]

The Carnegie Trust was also actively involved in attempting to improve and encourage opportunities for research at the Scottish universities. In 1905 its directors began to offer a number of fellowships, scholarships and grants. Fellows received £150 and were expected to undertake full-time research on their own, generally at an English or

8 Augusta Rudmose Brown, English assistant. *AM*, 28 (1910–11), facing p 17.

foreign university; scholars received £100 and usually worked under the supervision of their nominator at their own university; grants were smaller sums, generally awarded to permit research to be published. Professors recommended possible candidates from their own universities and then met to compare candidates and make a final selection. The number of research grants awarded annually tended to increase up to the First World War, but there was no fixed allocation by university, by subject, or by sex. Over the period 1905 to 1915 women were awarded just over a quarter of the fellowships and scholarships and less than 10 per cent of the grants. Aberdeen women graduates held a quarter of the scholarships and fellowships awarded to women and almost half of the grants, which, given the far greater number of women students at Edinburgh and Glasgow Universities, represented more than their share. Twenty-one female Aberdeen graduates received a total of thirty-five research awards, many of them for more than one year.[34] The Carnegie grants were an important avenue of advance for women, since Aberdeen University itself offered few scholarships and those established after 1864 had been ruled by the Commissioners not to be open to women.[35] In 1920 women were eligible for eight Aberdeen scholarships, ranging in value from £30 for one year to £200 for three years; and to another three scholarships open to competition between all the Scottish universities. Over the twenty-two-year period fifteen Aberdeen women were awarded twenty scholarships. As might be anticipated, many of these scholarship women also went on to study or research at the Oxbridge colleges.

In 1894 P J Anderson was appointed university librarian. Almost at once two women were appointed library assistants, though Anderson had been quick to deny a press report which implied that only women were being considered for the posts.[36] One of the assistants, Miss Best, was still working at the university library (as sub-librarian) in 1942. Neither Edinburgh nor Glasgow had appointed any female library assistants by 1904, by which time Aberdeen employed four—all paid less than their male counterparts. An even earlier appointment with Aberdeen University connections had been that of Elizabeth Christie, daughter of Professor Christie, as Organist and Director of Music at King's Chapel in 1891.[37] At a later date two eminent women scientists were appointed as examiners by the university; Marion Newbigin DSc, examined zoology from 1907 to 1909, and Helen Gwynne-Vaughan examined botany from 1913 to 1916.

In 1903 Johanna Forbes was appointed Latin assistant and two years later Mary Thomson (MA 1901) was appointed first assistant in the same department. Both women had graduated with first class honours in classics at Aberdeen and Mary Thomson had gone on to gain a first class in both parts of the Classical Tripos at Cambridge. Johanna Forbes' salary was £60 a year; Mary Thomson received £142. *Alma Mater*, which had declared Johanna Forbes one of the eight most prominent undergraduates the previous year, commented that it was 'a position the holding of which must be as great a trial for a lady as it is an innovation. We wish her in the name of the students all success.' Not surprisingly, Professor Ramsay's daughter recalled that there had been considerable hesitation about appointing a woman as a lecturer to the ordinary mixed graduating classes.[38] The experiment was sufficiently successful to be repeated and even publicised[39] but, as table 4 shows, the ratio of male and female assistants remained very uneven and the number of female appointments did not keep up with the increasing number of female students. Between 1900 and 1920 11.5 per cent of the assistants, 5.5 per cent of the assistants with the status of lecturer and 2 per cent of the lecturers were women.[40] The appointments lasted between one and four years and involved forty-seven women, most of whom were Aberdeen graduates. The concentration of female students in two faculties may have restricted the number of possible appointments, but in some departments sex discrimination played its part. Once women assistants had been appointed in a department, further appointments usually occurred over the next few years, but several departments were slow to take the first step until the shortage of suitable men as a result of the war and the high but short-term demand in the immediate post-war years, forced them to consider female appointments.[41]

As the experience of Augusta Rudmose Brown, appointed for four consecutive sessions, indicated, there was no possibility of promotion beyond assistant before the First World War, and even at the beginning of the Second World War only one woman was a university lecturer in her own right, though several women were, in practice, filling such positions. The first woman professor was not appointed until 1964, seventy-two years after the first women students were admitted. In 1989–90 there were again no women professors at Aberdeen.

The influence of William Ramsay, appointed professor of humanity in 1886, was evident not only in the appointment of the first women assistants, but also in the first female honorary degree, presented in 1895 to Jane Harrison, an eminent and radical classical archaeologist at Cambridge. The degree was reported to have received considerable publicity at the time, although it was not mentioned in her first biography.[42] A second honorary degree was conferred in 1899 on Anna Swanwick; principal of Queen's College, involved in the founding of both Somerville and Girton and a distinguished Greek and German scholar. This apparently exhausted the university's enthusiasm for recognising outstanding women. It seems surprising that not one woman was included, even in the long list of names brought forward in 1906 for the quatercentenary celebrations, considering that there were many women of academic note, especially at Oxford and Cambridge, who had never been awarded a first degree. Not until 1922 was a further honorary degree conferred on a woman—and Queen Mary was honoured as an institution rather than an individual—while degrees awarded after that date tended to be for service to the community rather than for academic distinction.[43]

TABLE 4 TEACHING STAFF AT ABERDEEN UNIVERSITY 1900–20

Year	*University Lecturers*		*University Assistants with status of Lecturer*		*University Assistants*		*Date of first female appointment*
	Male	*Female*	*Male*	*Female*	*Male*	*Female*	
1900	12	—			22	—	
1901	12	—			22	—	
1902	13	—	5	—	17	—	
1903	12	—	6	—	19	1	Humanity (Latin)
1904	13	—	8	—	17	1	
1905	14	—	7	—	19	2	
1906	15	—	8	2	18	—	
1907	13	—	9	1	18	—	
1908	18	—	9	—	23	1	
1909	18	—	10	—	23	1	English
1910	17	—	12	—	24	3	
1911	22	—	11	—	29	3	Modern Lang.
1912	19	—	9	1	33	—	
1913	22	—	11	—	30	1	
1914	24	—	11	—	30	2	
1915	25	—	7	—	28	4	Science
1916	26	—	7	—	25	7	Mathematics
1917	28	—	7	—	21	8	Philosophy
1918	29	1	9	3	27	9	Medicine Political Econ.
1919	42	3	5	1	20	10	Education Greek
1920	50	5	3	1	25	11	
	444	9	154	9	490	64	

9 Jane Harrison LLD. *AM*, 13 (1895–6), facing p 184

Chapter 5

University bursaries

Attendance at Aberdeen University was made possible for many students by the existence of a large number of bursaries, held for four years, ranging in value from £10 to £30. Some were offered by private patronage and some were restricted by geographical area or surname, but a large number (most of which were available only to arts students) were awarded by open competition, a competition which was keenly contested and carried great status throughout the north of Scotland. The University Commissioners' reorganisation of the university bursaries affected women students in two respects; first by the terms on which female students were admitted to bursaries, and secondly by the Commissioners' decision as to the subjects which should constitute the bursary examination and their respective weighting.

The Aberdeen University professors had clearly not envisaged the restrictions that were to be applied to bursaries. Before the ordinance, or even a draft version, had been issued on the subject by the Commissioners, the university had received an inquiry from Portsoy as to whether female candidates would be admitted to the 1894 bursary competition. Senatus had given a positive response, announcing that female candidates would be eligible to hold any bursaries except those from which they were specifically excluded by the deed of gift.[1] However, the draft ordinance issued in March 1894 only gave the universities the power to permit women to compete for those bursaries which had been endowed to the universities more than twenty-five years earlier, although the universities were also given the power to set some of these older bursaries aside for competition solely by women. But the ordinance advised that women were not permitted to enter for any of the bursaries instituted after that date unless they were expressly included in the terms of the foundation.

The Aberdeen Court objected to this interpretation and the male students, who had the most to lose, made a similar representation to the University Commissioners.[2] The graduate body of the university also repeated the view that all bursaries, scholarships and fellowships should be thrown open to competition among all students without restriction as to sex, on grounds of fairness and practicality, mixed with an anxiety that the quality of the long-established bursary competition should not be impaired:

> It seems highly inexpedient to detach bursaries from the General competition, owing to the difficulty of adjudging fairly the number and the values of those to be selected, there being at the same time no adequate knowledge of the field of claimants. The operation would be invidious in itself and could not fail to produce discontent and heart-burning on one side or the other.[3]

The Commissioners argued that they had no powers under the 1889 act to alter the foundations of any of the bursaries set up less than twenty-five years earlier and that, since women had not been admitted as university students at the time these foundations were endowed, they were, by implication, intended to be excluded, even if the actual wording of the original endowment was in general terms.[4]

Faced with these regulations, the Aberdeen University Court asked Senatus for advice on the best method of providing bursaries for women. The arts faculty did not suggest that any bursaries should be set aside for women only, but did recommend 'that all open bursaries which have taken effect prior to 30th August, 1864, should be offered for competition without restrictions to sex'.[5] When Edinburgh University asked Aberdeen if it would join with it in applying for the act of parliament necessary in order to enable women to hold post-1868 bursaries[6] the Aberdeen University authorities refused. Perhaps they felt the university held a sufficiently large number of pre-1868 arts bursaries (170 compared with 45 at Edinburgh) to provide for the additional students from this source alone. On the other hand, the University Commissioners were proposing to appropriate thirty-three of the Aberdeen bursaries and turn them into scholarships[7] and Aberdeen was the one university which had received no new endowments solely for the benefit of women students. Indeed, the nearest to such an endowment it was ever to receive was the Helen Scott foundation set up by Professor Trail in 1908 which was open to both men and women but 'of two applicants equally eligible but of different sexes the preference should be given to the woman (as more hampered by social usages)'.

The annual publication of the bursary competition results each year was an occasion for public discussion and analysis. The marks of the various percentiles were carefully compared with previous years and the number of placings obtained by rival schools were calculated as were other aspects such as the performance of town versus country schools, public versus fee-paying schools and later male candidates versus female candidates. As Lillie recalled:

> The boys of the Senior classes were entered for the annual Aberdeen university bursary competition. It had a great status significance, for all the clever boys from the schools of the North-East were entered and the attaining of the first place and the number of places attained by a school in the first hundred were matters of keen rivalry.[8]

The wording of this reminiscence was revealing; by the time the writer sat the bursary competition, girls had been entering the competition for nine years and twice, whilst he was a student, a female candidate gained the accolade of first bursar. However, Lillie aptly described the ethos surrounding the competition; he himself was a pupil of the Grammar School which traditionally vied with Robert Gordon's College for the greatest number of candidates in the first hundred places. Since neither school admitted girls, it was natural for them to have a male perspective of the competition, a bias which was encouraged by the fact that female pupils still accounted for less than a third of all the candidates.

The first six girls sat the bursary competition in 1894, before the new ordinance regulating it had been issued. The following year it was discovered that the highest placed woman was technically ineligible for a bursary because she had attended graduation classes in Latin during the summer. In view of the special circumstances of her case however, the bursary committee recommended that she should be given a discretionary bursary of a value corresponding to her position on the list.[9] As table 5 shows, female bursary candidates were consistently under-represented compared with the proportion of women students in the arts faculty, although since female students numbers were constantly increasing, the high proportion of women matriculating for the first time each year should have resulted in over-representation. Nor do the figures for those who passed the examination represent the number of women who actually held bursaries at the university. As was the case for men, a number of female pupils sat the competition more than once before finally obtaining—or accepting—a bursary.[10]

Male students noted the general improvement in the women's results with an understandable mixture of interest, pride, superiority and anxiety. A tradition of fair play and approval of hard work, combined in some cases with personal experience of competing against girls in the co-educational rural schools, meant that genuine praise and approval was forthcoming when the female bursars did well. But women's success in an examination long accepted as the most prestigious competition of the North East, shook the complacent belief held by many local men in the natural intellectual superiority of the male sex.[11]

TABLE 5 ARTS BURSARY COMPETITION[12]

Year	*Total no. of candidates*	*Total no. of female candidates*	*Female candidates as % of total*	*Female candidates as % of merit list*	*Highest placed female candidate*	*Female Arts students as % of all Arts students*
1895	163	11	6.7	10.3	15	10.8
1900	171	27	15.8	13.2	5	26.0
1905	149	35	23.5	27.0	8	39.8
1910	150	48	32.0	28.0	6	45.7
1915	154	71	46.1	43.1	11	63.0
1920	173	47	44.3	50.0	4	54.2

The ambivalent attitude of the male students was reflected in the student magazine which celebrated the arrival of the first female bursars with photographs and in 1896 commented that the most satisfactory fact about the competition that year was the high position taken by the women students; only fourteen had entered the examination but one (a village postman's daughter) had obtained seventh place overall and achieved the highest marks of the competition for mathematics.[13] It was typical however, that *Alma Mater* could not end without adding facetiously that the results 'boded well for further discomforture to the miserable male students at Kings'. A similar mixture of praise and sexist anxiety was evident most years. Although only a tenth of the candidates were female in 1897, *Alma Mater* commented that 'the progress made by women students in the last four years is considerable and the success of Miss Meta McCombie in gaining the 4th place this year is just one more sign of the gradual ousting of the wretched male'. The paper went on to list the place and percentage obtained by the leading female bursars since 1895 adding that it would 'always welcome those who go there with no fear of a little hard work whether of the gentler or sterner sex'.[14] In 1901 when female candidates gained first and third places in the 'Comp' and fourth-year women took several of the university classical prizes, *Alma Mater* referred to the invasion of man's domain 'by those whom ages of dominion have taught him to regard as his intellectual inferior—the so-called weaker sex . . . If their masculine rivals cannot win in open competition, they do not deserve greatly to be pitied'. But the paper showed ill-concealed relief the following year when 'the male was returned to his proper place'.[15]

Under the new ordinances the bursary competition was amalgamated with the arts preliminary examination. Candidates could take a maximum of five subjects for the bursary competition; mathematics, English and Latin were compulsory and these three subjects and Greek carried twice as many marks as the other options, French, German, Italian or dynamics, so that the maximum possible number of marks could only be obtained by taking both Latin and Greek. The distinction was made quite deliberately by the Commission, and indeed, if two of the Commissioners had had their way, Greek as well as Latin would have been a compulsory subject for both the preliminary and the bursary examinations and in the arts curriculum.[16]

Aberdeen was the only one of the four universities to object.[17] Both Senatus and the General Council wanted the system of marking altered, though their objections were not supported by the two professors of Greek, Principal Geddes and John Harrower. Even William Ramsay, professor of Latin, voted against the draft ordinance; not because he disagreed with the perceived academic value of classics, but because of the unfair means by which this was to be achieved. What might be fair as a means of testing ability to undertake a course was not considered fair for a competitive examination which would handicap some of the entrants from the start. Aberdeen's objections fell on deaf ears however and, indeed, may have had the opposite result from that wished for. So strongly did the Commissioners feel about the importance of the classics that they ensured that the ordinance controlling the bursary competition subjects and marking system could be altered only by another ordinance and the concurrence of all four universities.

The weighting of the marks naturally resulted in most candidates for the bursary competition choosing Greek as one of their optional subjects and encouraged the local schools to concentrate on the classics rather than on modern languages. The leading boys' schools in the town had long done so, but the classics, particularly Greek, had never been part of the girls' curriculum. Very occasionally girls attending co-educational schools had been taught Greek—in 1884 for example, five female pupil teachers from elementary schools in the North East had presented themselves for the annual Greek examination in connection with the Donaldson bequest[18]—but as Mackie had indicated, the secondary schools for girls in Aberdeen and the towns of the North East did not teach Greek or even advanced Latin. The experiences of one of the first female candidates (from Albyn Place School) aptly summarised the general educational difficulties facing the early women, yet she was one of the luckier students whose parents could afford extra tuition and were prepared to pay for it:

> Leaving school with only a smattering of Latin and no Greek, I spent a year under a private tutor, worked hard to pass the Preliminary Examinations and only after several failures succeeded. I even ventured to sit the bursary competition, and although I came out nearer the bottom of the list than the

> top, no matter for that I was the proud possessor of £10 per annum for four years, to which, for good behaviour, I got an additional £6 at the end of my course. In spite of being handicapped by an insufficient grounding, and by having to get up subjects so rapidly that they were by no means a possession for ever, there was great satisfaction in being one of the first girls at the university.[19]

It was possible for female students to enter the university and even to obtain bursaries without taking Greek. They were, however, unlikely to obtain high marks if they did so and many of the country schools which took both boys and girls were already involved in this rivalry and had suitably qualified teachers who could extend their classes to take in the female pupils in the school who had previously been taught modern languages. The intense pressure engendered by the bursary competition was recalled by pupils in the top class at Fordyce Academy:

> absolutely every boy had to take English (with History), Mathematics, French, Latin, and Greek; every girl had to take all these, except that for Greek she might substitute German,—but as German counted only 200 marks in the 'Comp.' as against 400 for Greek, German was frowned upon, or at best was tolerated as a poor relation.[20]

These were the only subjects ever studied during a school day that started at 8.30 a.m. and officially finished at 4.00 p.m., though as one old girl recalled, pupils were often kept in longer for extra work or to rewrite a Greek or Latin prose. Then after walking (or at a later date bicycling) several miles home, pupils started on homework which usually took till after midnight. Near 'Comp' time this was supplemented by a 'voluntary' session held at 7.00 a.m. on Saturdays to read the Odes of Horace, the headmaster usually attending in his dressing gown.[21]

The indigestible curriculum, long hours and absence of cultural activities, not to mention the largely male staff, created an educational system which Miss Buss and Miss Beale would certainly not have approved. Nor did the heads of the private Aberdeen schools approve. Whether because of the heads' dislike of the classical bias or the competitiveness, their determination to have a shorter school day or a curriculum more occupied with 'feminine' subjects, or simply because they thought it beneath the status of ladies to earn wages or win bursaries whereas men might, the result was that only a handful of girls from the private Aberdeen schools entered the competition, though their brothers at the Grammar School and Robert Gordon's College entered in large numbers. So it was not surprising that although 60 of the 96 candidates on the 1898 merit list came from Aberdeen city schools, only two of the eleven girls on the list did so, the remaining nine girls coming from eight different rural co-educational schools.[22]

The new bursary regulations came into effect in 1895. Four years later it had become accepted that it was necessary to take Greek to obtain a high position in the competition, and that year 99 per cent of the male candidates did so. But a larger number (and a far larger proportion) of female candidates did not take Greek, especially those educated privately or at girls' schools. The student newspaper began to examine the effect of the differential marks for the optional papers on the placings of the female candidates or, as it expressed on one occasion, the effect of 'handicapping' many of the candidates by 200 marks.[23] The position of the women was one of the major factors in furthering pressure for change but it is doubtful whether the reaction at Aberdeen would have been so strong if the new regulations had not had built into them a system of inequality. The question of justice was seen as a fundamental issue more important than the question of the relationship between classics, English and modern languages in school and university curricula. The general view was that, although Greek deserved to receive more credit than French or German, the existing examination system was nevertheless 'unjust and indefensible'.[24]

In 1899 Dr Scholle, lecturer in French and German, read a paper to the Scottish Modern Languages Association showing the effect of the current marking system on the results of the Aberdeen bursary competition. He quoted the example of two women students who had improved their placings by thirty and seventy-five places respectively when they substituted Greek, learnt in one case for eight months and in the other for a year, in place of a modern language learnt for several years. Copies of Dr Scholle's paper were forwarded to the university accompanied by a statement from the association declaring that the bursary ordinance allowing some of the candidates to compete for a higher maximum number of marks than others was 'unjust in itself'. Furthermore, it was asserted that, because it was almost impossible for candidates to obtain a bursary unless they took Greek, pupils in the boys' schools were being taught two classical languages and either one modern language or dynamics, while in the girls' schools and the larger number of mixed burgh schools, the girls were beginning to study Greek instead of German or French.[25]

The extent to which this was true is indicated in fig. 1. The number of female candidates in the bursary competition was small enough for individual variations to affect the overall pattern, but the increasing proportion of female candidates who took Greek is evident and, by 1909 when the ordinance was altered, over 75 per cent of female bursary candidates had chosen this option in two successive years. The extent to which the university curriculum was drawing local girls from modern languages to classics can be seen by comparing the bursary competition trend with that for successful candidates for the Aberdeen Higher

10 The sixth form at Fordyce Public School, 1898. D G M'Lean, *The History of Fordyce Academy*, p. 132. Nine of the girls sat the bursary competition; eight of these passed the university preliminary examination; six graduated (four with Honours) and Johanna Forbes was subsequently appointed a university assistant. Father's occupations included two farmers, two blacksmiths, an auctioneer, shoemaker, carpenter, slater and baker. One graduate married an Aberdeen graduate.

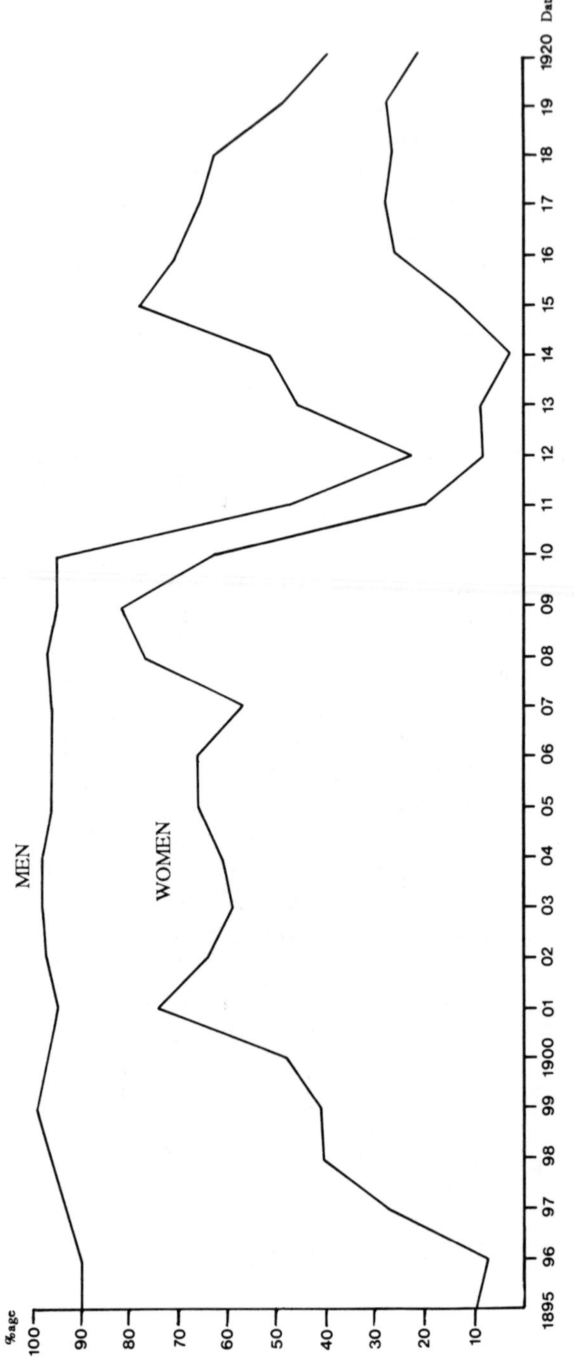

Figure 1 Selection of Greek at the Bursary Competition

Certificate for Women over the same period. Between 1894 and 1911 almost 300 girls took Greek in the bursary competition but none of those taking the Higher Certificate for Women during this period selected Greek and only one girl passed Latin whereas 128 passed French and twenty-one passed German.

The restrictive influence of the Scottish universities' bursary competitions as constituted led to numerous petitions on the subject from a wide range of bodies throughout Scotland. It was argued that the classical strait-jacket was restricting the development of the newly established English and modern languages honours schools in the Scottish universities[26] and preventing the development of a 'modern' curriculum with a commercial bent which would meet the demands of the community and so draw in more students.[27] Few of the institutions were likely to have been directly concerned about the position of women, though the modern languages associations obviously found them a useful point around which to base their arguments; within a university context the two aspects were related because of the greater proportion of female students who studied modern languages. It was frustrating for the embryo modern languages department at Aberdeen to see the best potential pupils either being drawn off altogether into classics or, by concentrating on Greek in order to gain a high place in the bursary competition, denying themselves the grounding in modern languages available at their schools which would have enabled them to go on to study honours at the university.

Despite the inter-relationship of these two aspects of the bursary examination question, there was no attempt by the university authorities to see them as a single problem, nor to impute to those who wished to see the old system changed a desire to bring 'women's education' into the university at the expense of the more important 'male' subjects. Nor was it ever suggested in public that women needed the 'soft option' because they could not cope with the rigours of a classical curriculum. The male students themselves were now choosing a wide variety of options and in 1908 the regulations were altered again so that it became possible to take an arts degree without studying either Greek or Latin, though one classical language was still required for the entrance examination. Furthermore the first women students had shown that they could, if necessary, study Latin and Greek as successfully as the men despite their later start in the subject and the rising standards. The male students admired them for this, particularly because of their continued belief in the greater intellectual difficulty of the classics; *Alma Mater* always made a special reference to any achievements by women students in what it described as 'the essentially masculine preserve of the Ancient Classics'.[28]

The resolution that had been presented to the university authorities by the Glasgow and West of Scotland Joint Committees was worded in such a way as to enable a separation of the question of 'fairness' from that of the relative merits of modern and classical languages. Equality in the total number of marks possible could be achieved either by taking a set number of subjects all carrying equal maximum marks—which would imply equality of subject matter—or by taking an optional number of subjects with varying maximum marks which when combined produced the same possible overall maximum, which would mean Greek could still be awarded twice as many marks as a modern language.

The Aberdeen arts faculty reported in favour of the second scheme, thus implying its belief in the greater intellectual difficulty of Greek and Latin. Dr Scholle supported this choice saying that 'it would remove our principal grievance, and still allow the Hellenists to look down upon French and German as an inferior subject—which would please them greatly.' Grierson, professor of English, was less diplomatic: the real point was that putting French and German on an equality with Greek would be fatal to the study of Greek.[29] Senatus considered the matter and resolved 'that the maximum number of marks obtainable in the bursary competition should be the same for all candidates', despite the objections of Geddes and Harrower. The University Court requested figures for the number of students who after taking Greek in the bursary competition, then went on to take Greek classes at the university and having considered these came to the same decision.[30] Aberdeen contacted the other Scottish universities to see whether they would consider making a joint approach to petition for an alteration to the ordinance. Meanwhile the Aberdeen General Council committee pointed out that there were twenty-three open bursaries founded since 1864 which were not subject to the ordinance and that the university could therefore award those, experimentally, on the basis of equal marks for all subjects without asking for further powers.[31] Senatus considered this suggestion but reported back that none of these bursaries were open to women students 'whom chiefly it is desired to benefit' and that only three of them were open to absolutely unrestricted competition. In view of this and the practical inconvenience that would arise from introducing two separate schemes of marking it was decided not to make any changes, especially since the entire question of the bursary competition regulations was currently under consideration by the University Commission.[32]

A special ordinance permitting the Senatus of each university to frame new bursary regulations received the Royal Assent in 1908. The following year the Aberdeen Senatus announced that henceforth marks for each of the eight subjects in its competition would have an equal maximum. The initial response was an enormous drop in the number of both men and women sitting the Greek option. But although a substantial minority of male candidates chose thereafter not to take the subject, the majority continued to do so. The drop in the number of women was greater, but about a quarter of the female bursary candidates continued to take the Greek option between 1915 and 1920.

The University Commissioners had remained powerless to alter the regulations affecting the post-1868 bursaries and although in the case of Aberdeen, this prohibition affected a relatively small number of bursaries, it nevertheless remained problematic, especially as (for the same reason) only one of the private patronage foundations was open to women.[33] Despite inter-varsity SRC conference motions, post-1868 bursaries were still open only to men (unless they specifically mentioned women) in 1920.

Chapter 6

Student Life

Physical provision and university supervision

Engaged in discussing the new ordinances and coping with such far-reaching effects as the changing functions of the Senatus and University Court, a new faculty of science, the introduction of modern languages and major alterations to the arts and medicine syllabuses, as well as with the dislocation caused by the work on the extension to Marischal College, the university authorities had little time or thought for the more practical problems that might accompany the arrival of female students. A consideration of the matter was precipitated by an inquiry from the principal of St Andrews University as to whether any arrangements had been made at Aberdeen for the supervision of female students. Senatus hastily established a committee to consider the matter.[1]

The committee recommended that the superintendence of the women students should be the responsibility of the existing house committees of King's College and Marischal. A special retiring room for women should be provided in the new buildings at Marischal and in the meantime it was suggested that they could use one of the library rooms,[2] while King's women entering that year as private students were allocated part of the men's cloakrooms. Such arrangements may seem trivial but as the library had no study facilities and there were no student recreational facilities available, such accommodation as was provided by the university was all that was available for students waiting between lectures.

The Senatus committee also recommended that the question of organising residential accommodation for the female students should be considered. This reflected a concern that women should have closer supervision and perhaps more attractive facilities than those to be found in the student lodgings used by men. More specifically, it was prompted by the belief that female students (especially those from upper middle-class families) were applying to the universities in the south rather than to Aberdeen, because of the lack of such facilities.[3]

In the 1870s the question of residence had been an important aspect of the debate over women's higher education. The amount of private hospitality available was limited and 'no real "lady" could take lodgings'.[4] Attitudes had begun to change by the turn of the century, and perhaps were always rather different in Aberdeen, though the difference there may have consisted more in the belief that girls who were not ladies should have an opportunity to study at university rather than the view that young ladies could now take lodgings with propriety. Almost no upper-class girls attended the university and it would appear that few upper middle-class girls did so unless they were living with their families or relatives.

The move towards residential accommodation for Scottish students was not restricted to women; the importance of students' social life was being emphasised from the 1880s onwards, and influential bodies such as the Carnegie Trustees and the University Grants Committee stressed the value of residential accommodation.[5] At Aberdeen, such proposals were never taken up very wholeheartedly, chiefly from a lack of funds; but they were also attacked by those who saw them as an expense which would prevent poorer students from being able to attend. This was the immediate reaction when the intention of the Aberdeen authorities became known in 1896. The women students' debating society voted against the idea and a male contributor to *Alma Mater* argued that although female students might gain from the social life of such an institution, only the wealthier women students would be able to afford such accommodation unless the cost was subsidised by benevolent individuals. Living in lodgings was not such an unpleasant experience as 'many well meaning but misinformed individuals' were inclined to think, and it would be better for women students that 'the spirit of independence should be asserted by roughing it, if needs be' than that they should become recipients of charity.[6]

Despite such objections, the business committee of the General Council listed residential accommodation for both male and female students as one of the major needs of the university and the Chalmers Trust provided funds to aid the establishment of a residence for women students which would be unofficially connected to the university. A committee of ladies was formed, headed by the principal's wife, to supervise the project and a lady from 'an old Aberdeenshire family' (her appropriate status thus delicately indicated) was appointed as lady warden. Castleton House, situated in the Chanonry near King's College, was purchased, prepared and advertised in glowing terms. It was suitable for quiet relaxed study, provided close access to the King's College classes, library and chapel, and it was also near the tennis courts, the recreation grounds, the ladies' golf course and the tram service for New

Aberdeen. But despite a reference by the principal in his graduation address not a single application was received from any of the 93 women students. Later in the year Lady Geddes held an 'at home' for female students at the residence. The function was well attended, but it was not successful as a recruiting campaign. Castleton House stood empty for two years before finally being rented out to a professor's family.[7]

> The secret of the failure of the hall of residence scheme is, without doubt, to be found in the Scottish girl's love of freedom and independence, and her idea that if the male students live in rooms—as they all do in Aberdeen—so should she.[8]

It does seem likely that the female students were glad of the chance to choose their own rooms and live 'unfettered by the rules and regulations inseparable from life in a hall of residence'. The prospect of being supervised by seven of the daunting professors' wives and sisters, and of being under the constant surveillance of a lady warden cannot have endeared itself; still less the requirement that each intending resident should produce both a certificate of health signed by her doctor and a character reference. But few upper middle-class families would have permitted their daughters to attend under any less strict regulations.

The other criticism of the proposed residential accommodation had been that the fees were too high 'for the class of girls who form the majority of the students'. This was probably an even more decisive factor in discouraging applications. The charge for board and lodging had been set at 21*s.* a week, or 26*s.* for an individual room exclusive of laundry charges and doctor's fees. But lodgings (usually including all meals, though the houses seldom had bathrooms) could be obtained for almost half the price, especially when two shared digs. Even in 1911, when 15*s.* a week was a normal rent, one student and her brother had digs in Dee Street for the princely sum of 12*s.* 6*d.*[9]

Many of the lodging houses were as much of an institution as the university itself; in some cases the same house had provided student lodgings for more than a century. Landladies rented out either to male or to female students; to have had both sexes in the same digs would have been considered very improper unless they were brother and sister. The nearest thing to an official residence during the pre-war days was a large house opened in 1905 near King's College where one of the female university assistants stayed. There, it was reported, the girls could have more of a home-life and greater comfort than was possible in lodgings for the 'moderate' charge of 15*s.* 6*d.* a week.[10]

Proposals to introduce residential accommodation in 1906 were criticised by one graduate as an attempt to anglicise the university. He suggested that residential accommodation was unsuccessful in Aberdeen because students had neither experience of boarding schools nor the funds necessary for residential accommodation. Whereas the English looked to collegiate life to develop independence and character, the Aberdonians considered that living in digs developed these traits. By 1914 the mythology of the female students' life in lodgings was well established and when the women students discussed whether hostels should be established, the loneliness of digs and the influence women could have upon each other was contrasted with the loss of freedom and the juvenile and narrow outlook residential accommodation encouraged.[11]

Another scheme was considered by the university in 1911 at the request of the Provincial Committee for the Training of Teachers which wanted to erect halls of residence for those of its female students who were not residing with parents or relatives. As a considerable proportion of the students for whom the committee was responsible were attending the university, it was hoped the university would support the scheme. The university subcommittee appointed to consider the question expressed polite interest in the idea, but refused to give any firm support until a definite proposal was presented, and lacking university backing the plan collapsed.[12]

During the war some of the graduates again became enthusiastic about promoting the corporate student identity and providing opportunities for social and intellectual exchange through residential accommodation; arrangements elsewhere for both men and women were carefully inquired into, and the General Council recommended that Aberdeen University should combine with the Provisional Committee as Edinburgh had done. The idea was criticised in *Alma Mater* on the grounds that it would not only check the development of co-operative student life but 'reverse the progress of co-education',[13] although ultimately it was again lack of funds which prevented further development. In 1919 Aberdeen and two of the London colleges were alone in not providing any residential accommodation for women students; over half of the Aberdeen women lived in digs—a proportion not closely matched by any other university.[14]

Student teachers were traditionally considered more immature and from a lower social class than university students. They were therefore seen as in greater need of supervision, especially in the case of women who were being trained to set an example of middle-class morality before working-class girls. Consequently the Aberdeen Provincial Committee not only attempted to establish residential accommodation for both its graduating and non-graduating students,[15] but also appointed a lady superintendent 'to improve the social well-being of the students, to foster habits of self-respect, and to raise the general tone of the college to higher levels'.[16] It checked the list of suitable lodgings, and drew up a set of rules for women students in digs. The students had to be in their rooms by 10.30 p.m. unless they had previously informed their landlady that they would be out late, in which case they could stay out until midnight, and they were not permitted to have visits from young men, unless they were relatives, without permission from the director of studies or the lady superintendent of the college, and then only until 8 p.m.[17] These rules may have been the unofficial standard of other university women living in lodgings, but the university as such did not draw up any formal set of rules. University students mocked the 'grandmotherly legislation' which had been introduced by officials in the Welsh colleges, prohibiting even conversation between the sexes in the college quadrangle and forbidding men to accompany women students to or from the colleges.[18] At Aberdeen, in contrast, the men always saw women home because they had to walk; there were no buses, only the circular tram, and it was customary for students to walk everywhere. A graduate living in King's Gate recalled that it took her twenty-five minutes to walk to Marischal (where there was invariably an eight o'clock science class) and thirty-five minutes to King's; in the summer she could cycle, however.[19]

Regulations were even stricter at Oxford and Cambridge, where the women students attended the universities on sufferance rather than by right, because of the fears of the officials in the women's colleges that perceived misdemeanours by any of the women would be used as an excuse to withhold such university privileges as had been granted to them. Thus in 1902 Newnham students were forbidden to talk to men in the street, and it was not until 1919 that the college authorities decided it was unnecessary for them to be chaperoned when entering a tea shop with a man. An Aberdeen graduate who went on to Somerville was astonished to find she was not permitted to invite her male cousin to dinner even though she was living with eleven other women students.[20]

At first the Oxbridge colleges had also been strict about chaperones at lectures and at St Hughes the practice continued until 1909, but it was never considered a necessary requirement at Aberdeen. When two women students attended their first botany lecture in 1892, a professor's wife and her sister went along to provide moral support rather than from any feeling that a chaperone was required, only to find the women already comfortably established in the front row of the lecture room. The solitary woman medical student of 1896 attended classes at Marischal without a female companion, and when timetabling prevented a pre-war science student attending one of the classes, she was given unchaperoned personal tuition.[21]

With limited public transport, and with university societies held only on Friday evenings, the women were often 'in'. Indeed, some landlords preferred male students as lodgers because they did not spend so much of their time at their digs. Life was not all work however. The digs of the Macleods, a Stornoway brother and sister who were leading participants in a number of student societies, were described as being 'as much a centre of university life as the Union'. Another student recalled how in 1909:

> some of us Bajanellas used to meet together in the digs, and would laugh and dance till our hair, insecurely braided in those days fell loose and untidy, and how the landlady would come and ask nervously if one of us would hold up the back of the sideboard lest it should fall, and we did hold it up too, but could not dance any longer for laughing.[22]

But there were also hints of real loneliness: one rural student reported that she had nothing to do but watch the trains go past, while another wrote of 'an attack of hysteria of loneliness' at night.[23] Meanwhile, the large proportion of female students who lived at home centred most of their social life and friendships around their family, neighbours and local church, rather than university activities.

The two Aberdeen colleges were separated by tradition and distance. More activities took place at Marischal, especially after the addition of the Mitchell extension in 1900, but the majority of women students were involved in arts subjects, predominantly English and modern languages, which were based at King's. There were few student facilities at either college. At Marischal the women were provided with a windowless room popularly known as 'the dungeon' or 'coffin'. At King's, the rapid increase in female student numbers created problems. By 1897 the accommodation provided was painfully inadequate; a room comfortable for ten or twelve was being used by sixty or seventy. Women ended up sitting in the cloakroom or even on the floor. A plea was made by one woman student for two small rooms: 'one for the regular students qualifying for graduation, and another for the private students attending one class, who do so much to make up the numbers, and yet have not the same need of accommodation'.[24] The following year the SRC urged Senatus to increase the accommodation for women students at King's and in 1899 a new retiring room was provided. However, heavy usage and the continual increase in female student numbers meant that history was soon repeating itself. In 1904 a complainant reported that the number of coat pegs was grossly insufficient, the wash basin needed repair, the towel was dirty, there were pools of water on the floor and the heating had effectively given up. There was a temporary improvement when a new room was triumphantly inaugurated with a tea party, complete with a hired piano.[25]

THE BAJANELLA.

THE TERTIANA.

11 The Bajanella and the Tertiana. *AM*, 31 (1913–14), p 178.

The women students' community

The physical condition of the women's room had its effect on the informal social relationships of the women students; the converse was perhaps also true. A wartime correspondent criticised the lack of sociability and camaraderie amongst the women at King's as compared with those at Marischal where 'functions' were held:

> A great deal in the meantime, must depend on the women and no power on earth could make the Ladies' Room an attractive or an inviting place. But if it became the custom for women to congregate there, women of different years and different tastes, the hideous crimson divan (of the broken springs) and the appalling array of hard straight-backed chairs would be forgotten . . . for the barriers of academic convention, that make women shy of the first advance to those older or personally unknown to them, are largely responsible for the depressing state of the Ladies' Room.[26]

The inadequate facilities and the absence of residential halls or a women's union meant that before the war the Women's Debating Society became a focal point for the association of female students: 'The first reports we ever heard of the WDS came from the girls who had older sisters at the Varsity. [It seemed] a flourishing and amusing society, that ever indulged in jolly "sing-songs" and informal "At Homes".'[27] But as a once-a-week activity the society had obvious limitations. The problem did not just affect the students; there was nowhere where the female university assistants or lecturers could meet either, and during the war three women members of staff had to arrange to have tea together one day a week in order to have informal discussions.[28]

In 1902 a female student, complaining about the 'temporary' common room available for women students at Marischal, suggested that the women might, meanwhile, be permitted to use the facilities of the Union. An editorial footnote in *Alma Mater* commented that the writer was wrong in suggesting that women were excluded from the Student Union and informed its readers that several female students were already members.[29] For the first few years after its formation the Union had been in dire financial straits as only a very small proportion of any of the students had become members. Several of the pleas for increased membership specifically included women, but only a small number of women attended classes nearby at Marischal and the facilities provided, including a smoking and card room and a billiard room, were aimed at male students.[30] By 1906, indeed, the Union was being seen by some members as representative of the 'genuine' (which was to say, male) spirit of the university which was in danger of being lost. The women enviously compared their own spartan facilities with those available at the other Scottish universities and articles began to appear recommending the formation of a separate women's union at Aberdeen:

> it would seem that our women students do not sufficiently realise what a potent factor in our university life is lacking so long as we have no Women's Union. To this is traceable the deplorable lack of public spirit which, it must be confessed, characterises the majority of the women students, but which under the circumstances, is scarcely to be wondered at. Only by frequent, free and easy social intercourse can we come by this spirit.[31]

The women students became increasingly enthusiastic about establishing their own centre at the university and after visiting post-war Aberdeen, the University Grants Committee described the women's facilities as 'lamentable' and recommended that priority should be given to this, rather than to the university's own proposals for residential accommodation.[32] The university finally purchased no. 52 Skene Terrace, using part of the funds provided by the Carnegie Trustees for improving the university's social life, and Griselda Dow (a wartime university assistant) became the first president of the Women's Union. But even this accommodation did not prove adequate, being too far from the university to become the social centre of the women students in the way that had been hoped.[33]

It had been suggested that the women students would have a better opportunity to develop an appropriate corporate spirit and administrative expertise if they had their own separate college,[34] but they rejected this idea. Some had made a positive choice in selecting Aberdeen, particularly the medical students for whom there were few bursaries and who usually came from families wealthy enough to send them to the southern universities if they wished; those who chose to study at Aberdeen in 1913 did so because they considered that the education provided for women at the separate medical colleges was not so efficient or comprehensive.[35] In the case of most of the arts students local connections and cheapness made Aberdeen the inevitable choice regardless of whether it offered single or mixed facilities. Possibly they feared poorer facilities in a separate institution, or simply felt it only just that their local university should provide for them too, for despite their relative lack of choice, women who went to Aberdeen were resolute in their opposition to the establishment of a separate college for women.[36]

Local connections also meant that many of the women arrived with some prior knowledge of what Aberdeen student life would entail through friends or relatives who had themselves attended. Of a sample of 383 women who graduated between 1901 and 1921, more than a third had at least one brother or sister who also graduated during that period

12 1909 King's College hockey match played between a team of eleven elder sisters and their eleven younger sisters. Thirteen of the women, including four pairs of sisters (and the two brothers who refereed), were Aberdeen graduates. Most were ex-Albyn Place or Aberdeen High School pupils. Six sat the bursary competition, four gained MA honours, three obtained both MA and BSc, five qualified as doctors, four married Aberdeen graduates. In contrast to illustration No. 10, father's occupations consisted of a university professor, an HMI, two ministers and five Aberdeen city merchants. AUR 35 (1953–4), p 49.

(although only five per cent were the daughters of Aberdeen graduates)[37] and it was not uncommon for an older sister to wait a year so that two sisters could be admitted to the university together. Social life was also influenced by the age of the students; the earliest university women were considerably older than their male counterparts—in 1900 most female students were 19 or 20 on admission and almost a fifth were 21 or over—but by 1910 most were 18 or 19, and by 1924 over half were 18 and a fifth were 16 or 17.[38]

Writing from a self-confident, intellectual, liberal, upper middle-class background, Mary Ramsay, the daughter of an Aberdeen university professor and sister of a woman graduate, summarised the ideal student community ethos for women:

> A true republican spirit reigns amongst the girl students. It is a republic based on intellect—wealth and birth are of no account therein. The girl of character and intelligence is the girl who is respected most, and most sought after. The snob is not tolerated. It is regarded, indeed, as a matter of duty that those girls who have the power should take their share in College life and their part in its responsibilities.[39]

Though the students themselves blamed any falling short of this ideal on the lack of facilities, there were two more powerful influences: strict emphasis on the accepted or conventional 'feminine' behaviour of girls and the social mores which controlled relations between the social classes.

Women's religious, school and family training emphasised from an early age that feminine behaviour should be submissive, supportive and passive.[40] As women who took the initiative became conspicuous and therefore by definition 'unfeminine', it was difficult to portray the social and political student activist as the ideal type of woman. On several occasions the minority of active male and female students bewailed the fact so few women were prepared to show any enterprise or initiative[41] but the majority of the women students remained more conventional.[42]

Nor did the women students form a socially homogeneous group, though comments about them often implied as much. Late Victorian and Edwardian Aberdeen society was composed of clearly defined hierarchical classes. Members of each knew their place and kept to it. Even within the middle class social conventions governed who would visit whom, who would speak first and the topics of conversation that were considered appropriate to the occasion. The professorial families were a part of the city's bourgeois elite and the behaviour of these women reflected the conventions; professors' wives 'visited' the wives of newly appointed professors but not the wives of lecturers, for example, and the Harrowers' ten-course dinner parties were famous.[43] Such social class distinctions permeated girls' education, especially in the city. The upper middle-class taboo that no one belonging to a lower social class might be invited home, with the corollary that they could not offer invitations in return, was enforced so rigidly that upper middle-class girls at the Aberdeen High School for Girls found themselves cut off even from their lower middle-class school companions.[44] Most daughters of professional or wealthy commercial or industrial families attended instead the more expensive and more socially exclusive private Aberdeen schools which prepared girls for the university. Meanwhile, the daughters of tradesmen and labourers attended the elementary public schools. The brighter or the luckier of those pupils went on to the higher-grade Central School established as a junior centre for student teachers, and some of the Central School pupils subsequently entered Aberdeen University as matriculated students, while a larger proportion attended the non-qualifying courses organised for student teachers.

In the country areas socio-economic distinctions were less obviously educationally divisive since parents who felt more strongly sent their daughters away to the secondary schools in Aberdeen or Edinburgh, and lower middle-class and even working-class girls might attend the network of rural higher-grade schools which prepared pupils up to university standard, alongside girls from rural professional and commercial families.

At the university all these women came together as students, but given the rigid class structure which they had been brought up to accept, it is difficult to believe that admission to the university resulted in an overthrow of the social conventions governing relationships between the social classes which applied even more strictly in the case of women than of men. In 1904 there was a reference to a distinct 'town' set and a 'country' set[45] and the influence of three of the all-girls secondary town schools, with their large numbers of university entrants and their higher social class, was evident in the fact that four of the first five women elected to the SRC were ex-pupils.

Relationships between university students and the non-matriculated student teachers are difficult to determine; some would have been sharing classes at the training college and others would have been previous school or neighbourhood friends. But the fact that a university student was criticised for bringing non-matriculated students to a debating society social evening[46] suggests there was little formal contact between the two groups.

Women student activists

> A girl can, of course, pass through a four-years' course and see comparatively little of her fellow students, and a hard-working and eager student has not very much spare time at her disposal. Still it is generally those who are the hardest workers and the best students who take the most active lead in societies, and the more social side of college life.[47]

A comparison of the sixty-nine women most active in student social affairs between 1894 and 1920[48] (see table 6) illustrates the considerable preponderance of middle-class women in such positions. Daughters of professional families constituted a quarter of the students but over half those prominent in student activities. Not surprisingly daughters of the manse and teachers' daughters were especially conspicuous, as both came from households with a tradition of voluntary social service by the women of the family. Women from non-professional middle-class families were slightly over-represented, whilst the daughters of farmers, tradesmen and working class families were under-represented. Few of those who did not go on to graduate became 'social elite', largely because there was a natural tendency for prominent students to be drawn from those who had been longest at the university. Rachel Annand was an exception, and criticisms of her may also have contained an element of class prejudice though this was never explicit, as her father was not only a master mason, but an active trade unionist. A later student who worked as a 'gutting quine' during the vacation to pay her way through college was careful never to mention the fact. But although there may have been informal snobbery and cliques, the institutionalised ethic of the moral worth of the 'lad of parts' was adopted by the women to the extent that there is no recollection of any publicly-mentioned or even semi-informal disparagement of lower middle-class or working-class women students comparable to that openly expressed at Cambridge.[49]

Student societies

Participation in organised student activities was part of the student ethos and assiduous members of student committees were to be found in the crowded ladies' rooms during the first few days of the session canvassing for members. Involvement was not restricted to undergraduates; both graduate students and the university assistants, only a year or two older, and closer in status to the students than to the professors, took part. But despite the emphasis on the corporate student community only a minority of male or female students participated in student activities and

TABLE 6 FATHER'S OCCUPATION OF SOCIAL AND ACADEMIC ELITE OF ABERDEEN WOMEN STUDENTS GRADUATING 1901–1920 (PERCENTAGES)[50]

Occupation	*All students*	*Social elite*	*Academic elite*
Clergy	7.8	15.9	5.6
Law	.8	7.2	1.9
Medicine	1.9	5.8	7.4
Education*	8.8	14.5	20.4
Civil service†	1.5	7.2	—
Other	4.8	4.3	3.7
TOTAL PROFESSIONS	25.5	55.1	39.0
COMMERCE‡	12.6	15.9	14.8
INDUSTRY‡	2.7	2.9	3.7
FARMERS	20.0	7.2	7.4
CLERKS/TRADESMEN§	16.2	7.2	20.4
Skilled W-C	12.9	8.7	7.4
Unskilled W-C#	6.1	1.4	—
TOTAL WORKING CLASS	19.0	10.1	7.4
NOT KNOWN	4.0	1.4	7.4
Total (%)	100	99.8	100.1
Numbers in sample	(525)	(69)	(54)

Fathers who were deceased at time of their daughters' admission have been included under their occupations, where known.[51]

* includes higher education, HMIs and school teachers.

† Senior Civil Service only, plus officers in armed forces.

‡ Owners and managers only.

§ includes minor officials.

\# includes domestic servants.

it is easy to over-emphasise the importance of these for the average student, especially before 1900. At that time the Debating Society and the Choral Society had memberships of over a hundred; but the remaining societies were few and small. All societies met on Friday evenings, so that although some enthusiasts might progress from one society to another during the time available, the number of societies in which any student could play an active part was restricted. Outdoor sports were popular with the men, but the majority of students, absorbed in the business of learning, regarded other activities, if not with scant respect at least with scant interest.[52] Formal undergraduate activities therefore convey the attitudes, experiences and reactions of a minority of the male and female students. Up to 1910 women's relative involvement in student activities kept pace with the increase in the total number of female students, but thereafter the ratio of actively involved women (committee members and those giving papers or speaking at meetings) declined (figs 2 and 3).

It was scarcely surprising that the Literary Society was the first student society to admit women in view of the extent to which literary interests predominated amongst the female students. The first women joined the society in October 1894 and the following spring Rachel Annand gave a paper. In 1896 several female committee members were elected; there were women vice-presidents in 1895 and 1901, and Augusta Rudmose Brown was appointed president in 1902. The custom then developed of appointing two vice-presidents, one male and one female. Not until the war was a woman again elected president, but from 1915 to 1918 women filled all three positions.

Many of the women students attended Literary Society meetings, but there was criticism of the segregated seating and the rows of empty chairs between male and female students.[53] This division was exacerbated by the nervousness of the women about speaking in public. One society president felt it necessary to make a public apology for his over-enthusiastic attempt to persuade the women members present to contribute to the discussion, explaining that he had been under the impression that their silence was due to a 'natural bashfulness' which might be overcome if they received a cordial enough encouragement.[54] At the time the women's behaviour irritated the male students; only in retrospect did some of them appreciate the internalised inhibitions women had to overcome to speak in public.[55] As female membership grew there were also allegations that the women had 'taken over' the society. Miss Rudmose Brown refuted the charge, showing that membership by sex remained equal; if attendance at meetings was less equally balanced, this was hardly the fault of the women students. *Alma Mater* provocatively joined in the debate, suggesting single-sex societies might be preferable:

> We hear much of the number of women that there are in the Literary Society, and while we do not lay the blame of the undoubtedly 'stagnant' condition of that society at their door, we ask the question, 'Is a mixed society a success?' Is it not the case that in such a society there is a restraint on the part of both man and woman?[56]

Another writer was less reticent: 'We shall have to see whether common sense or crass folly gain the day, though in a society so infested with women probably the latter will prevail'.[57]

In 1906 Mrs Annand Taylor recalled that 'when we first appeared at the Literary Society we sat together in the front row and listened meekly whilst male orators discoursed with varying degrees of fluency. . . . But at

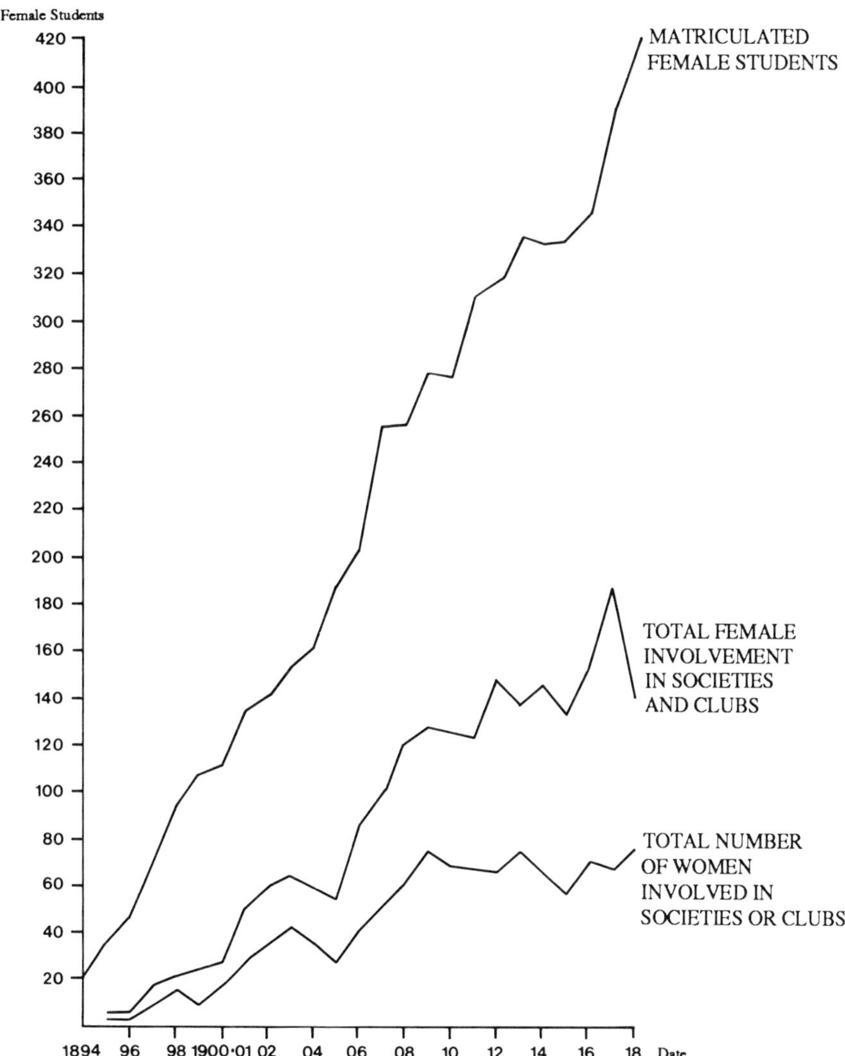

Figure 2 Women Students' participation in student societies and sports clubs

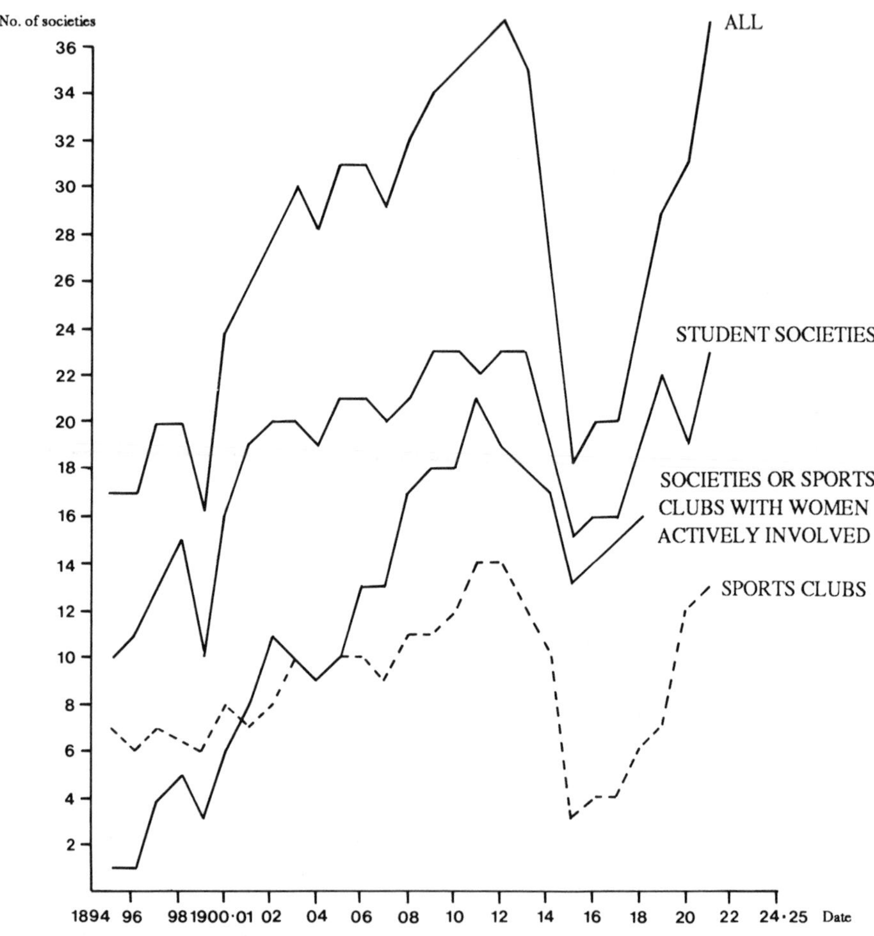

Figure 3 Student societies in which women participated

last we found voice, and now the Literary Society is hardly recognisable'. Despite her optimism an account of a 1908 meeting suggested that the difficulty remained. However, despite the problems, membership of the Literary Society continued to increase, leading in 1905 to the observation that the example of the Christian, Choral and Literary societies proved that mixed societies were the most successful.[58]

The University Choral Society combined the individualistic self-improvement ethos of the mid-nineteenth-century students and the tradition of bacchanalianism which expressed itself on such occasions as bursary night. The society had in fact been founded less than twenty years earlier (and after the Literary Society) but it had already developed hallowed traditions. Its image was continually reinforced by articles from graduates of the period describing its halcyon days; publication of the *Song Book* progressed into a veritable student industry, taking up more discussion time at Scottish Inter-Varsity SRC conferences than any other topic; and the yearly student concert provided an occasion which was analysed by the local press in almost as much detail as the bursary competition.

Sandford Terry, professor of history and biographer of Bach, saw the women as a welcome source of sopranos and altos which would enable the society to broaden its musical canvas and it clearly never occurred to him that the existing student members might not agree that musical criteria should have priority when he suggested that women should be 'allowed' to join the Choral in 1899. A leader in *Alma Mater* attacked his proposals on the grounds that it would alter the society's unique 'social characteristics' and make the club's merits dependent solely on its music which, it was argued, it would be difficult to maintain at a high standard in a society with a fluctuating membership. A few hopeful women attended the first rehearsal but on finding that they were not welcome did not repeat the experiment.[59]

Four years later Terry again proposed the admission of women. This time the issue was carefully debated in advance to avoid any possible repetition of the previous embarrassment and it was decided by a majority vote to admit women for a trial period. Not surprisingly this decision, which was largely the result of Terry's influence, was controversial; many members feared that the admission of women would lead to the society's decline. 'Some of the old members have gone, and others say they are not going to join.' One of the old school declared that: 'The university Choral Society under the leadership of Professor Stanford Terry was a male voice choir and as such an inspiration to the participants. When it became a mixed choir it lost its verve.'[60] It was indicative of the importance attached to the change that it was followed up by a leading article in *Alma Mater* on the 'recognition of women in the university'.[61] Professor Terry strengthened his position and women students were admitted not only to membership but also to the committee. Membership figures for 1906–11 showed an increase in female membership and a fall in male membership, but despite the forebodings the society survived and thrived—a graduate who matriculated in 1911 described it, with the same sense of excitement and tradition as her predecessors, as the outstanding pre-war society with an annual concert in the Music Hall to which 'everyone went'.

The Debating Society, which had discussed and rejected the higher education of women three times in the fifteen years prior to women's admission to the university, nevertheless made women politely welcome when they arrived, but only as outsiders. The women were invited to the debating finale where they observed an unpopular speaker:

> enveloped in a picturesque rain of cabbage. Had we not been there, worse things might have happened, we could only suppose. After that we sometimes attended special debates sitting in the galleries reserved for our use like medieval ladies at a tournament.[62]

It was in 1895 that the society passed a motion that members should occupy the lower part of the hall and the gallery be reserved for lady students and visitors. Thus the distinction between the two sexes was physically enforced.

At the beginning of the twentieth century the men's debating society found itself in financial difficulties, but only once was it seriously suggested that membership should be opened to women and then the proposal was quashed.[63] Once it had become clear that the society did not intend to admit women to membership in the foreseeable future, the women formed their own society. The Women's Debating Society, established in 1896, was an early indication of increasing self-confidence among the female students and of a determination to create their own social life if necessary. Each year an opening address was given by one of the professors' wives, often on the subject of female education and the social responsibility of the educated woman. The women students were inclined to discuss aspects of morality or personal character rather than wider social and economic issues. Occasionally, however, questions such as suffrage or separate education for women were considered and in imitation of the men's society a 'political evening' became an annual event. In 1906 Mary Ramsay commented:

> The Women's Debating society has flourished for many years. Girls who join no other societies often join this. They come into closer touch with each other here, and the older girls, as officials, meet and know the new recruits from town and country . . . [On hat night] the girls accustom themselves to expressing their views upon matters political, philosophical, and literary,

> without premeditation. . . . Early in the session the society gives an 'At Home'. Only girls are present, and with music, games, and dancing the evening passes all too fast.[64]

The society appears to have been better attended than its Edinburgh counterpart and the reports in the student magazine certainly give no indication of the preoccupation with membership numbers and procedure which was a feature of the Edinburgh society.[65]

At the beginning of the 1901–2 session the female students established a Women's Medical Society. It was a brave gesture at a time when there were only eighteen female medical students compared with 308 men, who could not resist joking about the new society. The group was frequently addressed by women doctors, who were able to advise the students in the light of their own experiences and who, for their own part, must have enjoyed having the support of a local group of sympathetic and like-minded women. There was special need for such mutual support in 1902 when the second woman to graduate in medicine at the university, winning the Lizars' medal for anatomy in the process and then obtaining the post of house surgeon and physician at the Sick Children's Hospital in Aberdeen, committed suicide.

13 Women SRC members, 1907–8. (Left to right) M R Forgan, Winifred M Gray, I L Coutts, Mary P Ramsay—Convener. (Front) Alice M M'Hardy. *AM*, 25 (1907–8), p 186.

Chapter 7

Student Politics

The Students' Representative Council

The issue of women's representation on the Students' Representative Council was raised as soon as matriculated women students entered the university[1] and in 1897 two female students were elected to the SRC. The following year another two women were nominated, but the candidacy of one was declared invalid and so the other withdrew.[2] No women stood for election during the next few years, although in 1900 a writer in the women's column tried to stir up enthusiasm: 'Everybody is asking why there are no ladies on the SRC. The fact is—although a few of us claim to be liberals, we are all conservative at core, and real blasé about innovations of that sort'. The Women's Debating Society voted in favour of women SRC representatives, but fear of conspicuous behaviour prevented any women from volunteering.[3] Although an article about women in the university ten years after their admission argued that they should have representatives on the council—'the sooner they come into their full rights as a power in the university, the more perfect will be our student life'—the women's lack of involvement had adversely influenced some male students' attitudes and the idea of separate representation for female students was raised in public for the first time: 'There is now at any rate a lack of conscious precedent to go upon, and probably it is not quite suitable for many reasons that women should compete with men in election by poll.'[4] A subsequent motion by one of the SRC members proposing 'adequate and official representation of the women-students' was narrowly defeated.[5]

A letter to *Alma Mater*, published in October 1906 when women constituted almost a quarter of the students, reflected the influence of the growing women's rights movement, which had impinged on the city that autumn:

> Women form a large percentage of the Arts students, and surely they should be properly represented. Men cannot do so. We thank them for what they

> have done for us in the past, but believe we could do the work better ourselves in the future. This is our right and if we cared, we women students could insist on it . . . Why should there, indeed by any opposition? Have not women proved themselves at least the equals of men in class work? Their business qualifications have been recognised in their election to the committees of all the societies where men and women students meet. There is a woman Vice-President of the Literary Society and of the Christian Society, while the affairs of the Women's Debating Society are most efficiently managed by women.[6]

This was followed by a conference of women arts students at Marischal where, after much discussion and some opposition, it was decided to nominate a candidate for the 1906 elections to represent each year of the arts students. The alternative proposal, to elect a committee which could then present women students' interests to the SRC, was rejected on the grounds that it would have no official standing and would leave women in the humiliating position of having to ask for a recognition which was theirs by right. The following week the entire leader of *Alma Mater* was devoted to the issue, beginning with an indirect reference to developments in the suffrage campaign: 'With us, as in London, women are seeking some control over affairs'. Others, less restrained, reported that it was 'the clacking mob of demented squawkers' which had influenced some of the Aberdeen students.[7]

Four of the women candidates were defeated and the single elected woman withdrew 'from a reluctance to be either the only woman in the Council or shirk the responsibilities of her position'. Opinion as to the advisability of women on the council was reported to have wavered during the elections. Some women who were opposed to it became supporters owing to the treatment the women candidates received at the heckling meetings, although an *Alma Mater* reporter considered most of the questions put to the women had been 'uncommonly practical and asked in a serious spirit of enquiry'. On the other hand, some men who had been inclined to favour the women's attempt were reported to have been alienated by the fact that in one of the constituencies two male students were nominated to split the men's vote. They may also have disliked the attempt to force their hand; the issue had become abrasive and sharply defined in terms of gender, with women students 'demanding' representation, rather than waiting for it to be offered as had occurred earlier.[8]

The resulting situation was obviously not satisfactory and *Alma Mater* suggested that the Aberdeen women should have a representative for each year, for which they alone would vote; the presence of women would undoubtedly be detrimental to the efficiency of the council, but it was not possible 'in all justice' to exclude them. It would be advisable, however, to ensure that the majority of the SRC would always be male.[9] The view that women should not compete with men for SRC positions recommended itself to the newly elected SRC, especially since the proportion of female arts students had increased sufficiently to sway the vote; one male writer even considered it would be better for women students to have no vote at all than for affairs to continue as they were.[10] The representation finally decided upon provided for five women representatives to be elected directly onto a council which would consist of forty-five members altogether; two even less generous proposals were withdrawn for constitutional reasons.[11]

Subsequently *Alma Mater* summarised the situation more calmly, noting that there had formerly been female SRC representatives but that at that date there were none for almost two hundred women: 'Although proportionate representation would have given them twice this number of members, they seem to be satisfied with what they have been granted. We venture to predict that they will soon be asking for more'.[12] Another writer suggested that women's sexual influence would give their representatives more impact in the council than their official numbers suggested.[13] Though the new constitution of 1908 was important for its symbolic recognition of women students' involvement in the affairs of the university, it proved to be a hollow victory:

> The last year's method of exclusion of women by the men would assuredly not have worked this year, seeing that in one or two years the women preponderate. So the SRC, none too late, have introduced a rule which will preserve the fair dominance of the men, and which will be sufficient safeguard against the disproportionateness of the numbers of women and men which shows itself this year and is likely to continue.[14]

It was clear where the SRC's priorities lay; an early motion that the Amusement Committee should consist of six male members obtained a large majority. It was not until 1912 that a woman was actually elected onto the committee and then there were complaints that she was ignored by the other members.[15] The assumption, sometimes explicitly stated, that the women representatives would only be useful in connection with matters specifically concerning the female students,[16] was carried into the early meetings. The first motion presented to the SRC by a female representative was that the ladies' room at Marischal should be made habitable, a matter which was duly referred to the female members of the council; the women representatives also pressed for improved physical training facilities to be provided for women students. At the end of 1908 *Alma Mater* noted with approval that the female representatives had

14 Mary Esslemont, SRC President 1922–23 *AM*, 40 (1922–23) p 144.

relieved the male students' burden by looking after the interests of their own sex, and that they had 'not made themselves the public nuisances they were expected to'.[17] Relations between the men and women SRC members were generally harmonious, but in 1909 a special meeting had to be called to deal with complaints by an exasperated Margaret Forgan that the SRC meetings were poorly attended, unpunctual and conducted 'with levity'.[18]

Two years later the female undergraduates did decide that they were insufficiently represented on the SRC, but a motion proposing increased representation and at least one representative of each sex in any faculty where there were both male and female students, was rejected by the executive. In 1911 women were allocated nine of forty-seven seats,[19] a proportion of 19 per cent at a time when they constituted over 27 per cent of the student population. In 1916, when women students actually outnumbered men, their representation was increased to twelve places. Not until after the war was proportional representation introduced.

The first woman president of the SRC was Mary Esslemont, elected in 1922. She had graduated in science in 1914 and arts in 1915; had been appointed a war-time university assistant and after the war became a student of medicine. Older than the male students who had remained at the university and more in contact with university affairs than those whose studies had been interrupted by the war, she was an obvious choice. But although she later claimed to have experienced little personal animosity, the election meeting itself was a stormy affair. First it was suggested that the votes of absent SRC representatives should be recorded and then that election should be by ballot. Both these moves being defeated, an alternative candidate was put forward with 'a prolonged eulogy'. When Mary Esslemont was elected despite this (by 26 votes to 15) two of the men requested that 'their dissent to the election of a woman as President be recorded in the Minutes'.[20] and a disapproving Eric Linklater later told her that her appointment had 'split student opinion'. Her appointment also caused consternation to the professor who convened the Chapel Committee:

> He said to me when he heard, you see, that I was elected president, 'Of course you won't read the lesson'. The reaction of the SRC committee was, 'All right, if the President's not allowed to read the lesson, no kirking of the SRC'. So then I rang up the principal, G A Smith, and he said, 'Of course the president reads the lesson'.[21]

15 Procession of women students at quatercentenary celebrations, 1906. AUL, *Souvenir of Quatercentenary Celebrations.*

Women's suffrage

The issue of votes for women pre-dated women's admission to the universities, but not in any pervasive or serious fashion. The Debating Society rejected the proposed reform by a large majority in 1868;[22] that the debate was held at all reflected the extent of public controversy over John Stuart Mill's bill, but the subject was not considered again until 1884. After the admission of women to the university the male students debated the issue in 1894, when the motion was defeated by 39 votes to 26, and in 1900.[23]

The growth of a more serious student interest in political affairs in general at the turn of the century led to the formation of student Liberal and Unionist Associations, much to the delight of John Murray Gibbon, an ex-editor of *Alma Mater*:

> I am glad to hear that the members of my old university are beginning to take an interest in some subject that will not pay in examinations and that the petticoat invasion has not knocked all the manhood out of either King's or Marischal. For this political movement, I take it, has its origin in male brains, and the political clubs, I hope, will under no circumstances admit of woman's suffrage.[24]

Although many of the male students, particularly the Liberals, did support women's suffrage, the women were kept out of the mainstream political clubs. Liberal women formed an independent association in 1900 and two years later a Ladies' Committee of the Unionist Association Society was instituted. Despite this sign of political activity amongst the women students, they appeared even less interested in women's suffrage than their male colleagues. The first time the issue was formally raised in the Women's Debating Society was in 1905 when Mrs Trail chose to give a comprehensive summary of the arguments in support of suffrage as her address. A few months later the society had an animated discussion on the even more controversial issue of whether women were qualified to assume positions of responsibility in affairs of state, a proposal rejected by a majority of three.[25]

The following year the university was forced to take official cognisance of the issue; a general election appeared imminent and the Glasgow registrar contacted his colleagues at Edinburgh and Aberdeen to discuss whether the universities, as electoral constituencies, should issue voting papers to women members of their General Councils. The Aberdeen registrar considered that the universities should not do so because women were under a 'legal incapacity'. The Edinburgh registrar thought that it was the universities' duty to issue voting papers to all members of the

General Council regardless of sex, leaving the question of the right of female members to vote to be decided at the poll. In view of the uncertainty, Glasgow suggested that the three universities should share the cost of submitting the question for a legal opinion. Counsel agreed with the Aberdeen registrar, and consequently none of the Scottish universities issued voting papers to women at the 1906 General Election.[26]

Although a committee was established by women graduates at Edinburgh to appeal against this decision, the question of the suffrage rights of women graduates does not appear to have been much discussed by Aberdeen students at this date. Their awareness was aroused more forcefully when representatives of the Women's Social and Political Union (including Mrs Pankhurst) visited Aberdeen in the autumn of 1906 and then in the following spring during a by-election campaign in South Aberdeen. A tongue-in-cheek complaint by the male students that they had not been visited by the suffragette leaders campaigning in the city resulted in a visit to Marischal College by Annie Kenney and Helen Fraser, a good-humoured occasion commemorated in bad verse.[27] The broader issues raised by the women's campaign clearly influenced the female students' attempt to obtain SRC representation and the backlash reaction of conservative men to the more forceful and direct efforts of the women to obtain the vote played its part in their defeat.

In 1908 a majority of the Women's Debating Society voted in favour of separate spheres for the sexes—'man for the field and woman for the hearth'. But other views were also evident in the university. A letter to *Alma Mater* complained about 'votes for women' badges being worn in chapel and the Aberdeen University Woman Suffrage Association was formed, rather surprisingly pre-dating a similar association at Edinburgh University. Membership, open to both male and female students, indicated support for the principle of suffrage for women qualified to vote, not approval of the methods pursued by the Women's Social and Political Union.[28] Even so, the new society was not without its critics amongst both male and female students. One woman wrote in horror on hearing that the society was organising a meeting to be addressed by two national suffrage campaigners, Rosemary Gawthorpe and Helen Fraser, even though at this date the suffragettes had done nothing more unfeminine than hold public rallies:

> I hear the Votes for Women Association are to have a meeting soon, with addresses from some of the women who have been disgracing their sex recently. I am not sure of names, but I hope the good feeling and good breeding of my fellow students will prevent them from being associated with women who make the term 'lady' obsolete and who degrade every noble association which we connect with our sex.[29]

By this time, the Aberdeen students had learnt from the national press how suffragettes should be treated. The meeting, held at Marischal College led to the type of pandemonium more often reserved for the rectorial contests. Male and female ticket-holders had been admitted, but about fifty other male students gathered outside spoiling for a fight. They found a substitute for a battering ram and, bursting the doors in, invaded the meeting armed with handbells and whistles. At one point the noise was so great the speaker had to revert to the blackboard, a fight nearly started and a smoke bomb was let off.[30] A more measured indication of male student response came from the Debating Society where fifty students voted by a two-thirds majority against women's rights.[31]

The start of the next academic session saw activity over the rectorial election. There was already a tradition of female involvement at the rectorials; in 1896 Rachel Annand had been president of the Murison supporters and had spoken at a meeting on his behalf, and in 1899 there were female students on Lord Strathcona's election committee although they had not attended the celebration dinner laid on by the lord rector.[32] The 1908 election was of special relevance to the female students who had been drawn into supporting or opposing women's suffrage as a result of the events of the preceding year, because the Liberal students asked Asquith, already the target of the national women's suffrage parties as a result of his personal opposition to extending the franchise to women, to stand for election. The Unionist Party candidate was the Irish Conservative MP, Edward Carson. The more determined student supporters of the campaign for women's suffrage adopted the WSPU policy of opposing Liberal candidates and attempted to persuade other female students and male supporters of women's suffrage to vote for Carson. The rectorial election was therefore a parallel to the previous year's by-election in the city, although on this occasion the situation was made less complicated by Asquith's opposition to women's suffrage and Carson's guarded support.[33] *Alma Mater*, under the pungent editorship of R N Gilchrist, was not even-handed in its reporting:

> The female party was also abroad, vulgarly (the same adverb applies to the others too, but less frequently), in their dealings with their fellows, arresting young ladies and hugging them till one of their party had affixed their glaring, atrocious-looking badge. Surely the new lady students must resent the down-your-throat methods of the exuberant Suffragettes. They seem more like policemen arresting carters than civilised students canvassing their fellows. Asquithites and Carsonians both alike remarked on the unreasoning methods of the Shriekers.[34]

Like the other political student societies, the suffragists produced a campaign magazine, defiantly titled *The Suffragette*, comprising the usual mixture of squibs, cartoons, and poems, as well as messages of support from the three national women's suffrage societies, complaints about the party bias shown by *Alma Mater* and an article explaining the suffragists' opposition to Asquith, and the particular importance of indicating that opposition in view of his announcement a few months earlier that he would be influenced by evidence of women's support for the reform. The women argued that female liberal students who voted against Asquith would not be 'negating all their convictions for this one tenet' because the tenet in question was 'the foundation of all political principles'. Until women actually had a vote they were not political entities and had no effective means of influencing government measures.[35]

The AUWSA organised a highly successful 'cafe chantant' in the YMCA.[36] Patrons of the society who were present included Mrs Murray, wife of MP James Murray, who at that time was engaged in offering his personal assistance to the Pankhursts during their imprisonment, and the two most committed suffragists amongst the professors' wives, Katharine Trail who had addressed the women students on the subject before the Pankhursts had made it fashionable, and Lady Ramsay who had become president of the Aberdeen branch of the Women's Social and Political Union established the previous year. At the meeting Chrystal Macmillan, an Edinburgh university graduate and secretary of the Committee of Women Graduates of the Scottish Universities (Parliamentary Franchise) reported on the appeal to the house of lords against the refusal of the Scottish universities to admit women graduates as voters, on the grounds of their academic qualifications, alongside the male graduates. The subsequent decision against the women graduates was published on 10 December 1908.

Whatever the pre-election promises of individual students, the campaign of the student suffrage society was unsuccessful and Asquith was returned as rector. A detailed analysis of the voting showed that eighteen of the 246 women students did not vote while the remainder were divided almost equally between the two candidates, 115 votes for Asquith and 113 for Carson although since votes were actually counted by 'nations' the women's vote went to Carson.[37] Votes were cast in public and *Alma Mater* reported that those women who voted for Carson were recipients of considerable teasing. One wonders what difference a secret ballot might have made in a situation where ridicule was being used as a powerful means of persuasion. Students may also have been frightened of the reaction of the university officials; one student was warned by more conservative colleagues that actively campaigning for the militant suffragettes would result in her expulsion from the university: 'Of course there was nothing of the sort! The university authorities were most sympathetic'.[38] As most women were in the arts faculty, which was

16 Cartoon from *The Carsonian*, 5, 30 October 1908, p 6.

traditionally Liberal, it has been argued that the women's vote was considerably influenced by the suffrage issue, but male contemporaries did not interpret the results that way. The *Carsonian Review* commented that the suffragist leaders had worked very hard amongst the girl-students, but their labours had not been rewarded, few apart from the officials having the courage of their nominal convictions to vote against Asquith, though several had declared they would do so right up to the polling day. The president of the university Liberal Association admitted surprise that Asquith's attitude towards women's suffrage had not had a more prejudicial effect on the votes of the women Liberals: 'The attitude of the Women Liberals towards the Suffrage Question is in my opinion an emphatic answer to those who would have made female suffrage an issue at any Rectorial Election.'[39] The experience may have led Asquith to a similar conclusion at a national level.

The events surrounding the rectorial election resulted in widespread hostility towards the women's movement and student suffragists found themselves the object of public criticism and ridicule. The women's debating society voted against suffragist militancy; the men's debating society declared that the movement for women's rights was detrimental to national interests; a minister addressing the Celtic Society remarked that he would turn a jet of water on the suffragettes; and the Marischal College attendants wanted to refuse women admission to the forthcoming rectorial address. *Alma Mater* even criticised a female undergraduate for appearing at a public woman's suffrage meeting in academic dress: it might 'delude some people into the belief that students officially recognised the movement she herself represented'.[40]

But despite the hostility a minority of committed female students, such as Isabella Leitch and Agnes Mure MacKenzie, were actively involved in suffrage activities in Aberdeen City.[41] Supportive male students were evident too. The suffragette in student dress was defended by William Macleod, an ex-editor of the student newspaper and member of the Women's Suffrage Association. Male students often provided protection for women selling the suffrage paper, whether they wanted it or not; and one of the major incidents of suffrage vandalism carried out in Aberdeen in 1913, when 'Release Mrs Pankhurst' was cut in twelve-foot high lettering in the turf at Duthie Park, was done by male medical students.[42]

Activities also continued in the university. In 1908 a well-respected male student in drag interrupted the rectorial address. In 1910 graduate Helen Ogston addressed the AUWSA though, for reasons which will later become apparent, the authorities refused permission for a room at Marischal to be used. In 1911 a joint meeting of the women's debating and suffrage societies was held; that this was a debate about the means of obtaining women's suffrage, rather than whether such an end was to be desired, reflected a shift in many of the women's views, even though they still criticised militant suffragism. It was agreed by a large majority that it would be better to present a separate bill for the enfranchisement of women, than to incorporate a measure into an adult suffrage bill. At a joint debate with the Sociological Society the motion that 'the enfranchisement of women is the most urgent social need and should precede all others' was carried.[43] Frequent references to, and papers about, suffrage and women's rights, both comparative and argumentative, spilled over into student societies as varied as the Celtic, the Christian Union and even the Classical. One of the last demonstrations occurred in 1914, when a visiting minister was interrupted in the course of a lecture on 'the Christian ideal of justice' held in the Mitchell Hall. The horrified reaction of *Alma Mater* would have carried greater weight if there had not been a tradition of notoriously disrespectful behaviour by male students during prayers on formal occasions.[44]

Nevertheless, although individual students felt strongly on the issue, the majority remained uninterested in politics or suffrage, an attitude reinforced by the contemporary view in upper middle-class circles that politics were not respectable; and those intending to become teachers, as most of the women students were, had to be especially circumspect.[45]

Even in retrospect, suffrage supporters were divided over the effects of militancy. A leading non-militant argued that the activities of the militant suffragettes had delayed the vote. Interestingly, the most frequently quoted incident was wrongly attributed—but the error in itself reflected the local scandal it had caused at the time. Helen Ogston, an Aberdeen science graduate, daughter of the professor of surgery and sister-in-law of the professor of English, acquired a dog-whip to protect herself from sexual assault during suffrage activities and used it when she interrupted a speech by Lloyd George in 1908, an action notorious enough to earn her an illustration in *The Graphic*.[46] However, graduates interviewed informally in the 1970s confused this incident with an occasion four years later, when a suffragette thought she saw Asquith at Aberdeen railway station and rushing forward, proceeded to lay about him with her whip.[47] In reality, however, it had been Emily Wilding Davison, who was responsible for the second incident.[48] In any case, it proved to be a case of mistaken identity; Emily Davison was sentenced to ten days imprisonment, and when the baptist minister who was the unwitting recipient of her attack died of a heart attack three months later, his death was widely attributed to the shock of the assault. But whereas the non-militant suffragists believed that it was not militancy, but women working as munitions workers during the war who gained the vote for women, militant activists such as Isabella Leitch argued that without the impact of militant suffragism there would have been no such female munitions workers.[49]

The First World War

The outbreak of war turned the university into a predominantly female institution. The Aberdeen University Corps was mobilised immediately, and within a short time the only male students remaining were those studying medicine or the medically unfit, later to be supplemented by a third category—the war wounded.

Suffragettes were amongst the first to call for patriotic seamstresses and students were also asked to support the field hospital units established under the auspices of the Scottish Federation of the National Union of Women's Suffrage Societies. Myra Mackenzie, the first female medical graduate at Aberdeen, was one of the doctors serving with the units. Women students inquired whether the authorities would be prepared to grant the same concession to them as to men on active service; in 1915 the first female student left to take up munitions work, and one of the library assistants obtained leave of absence to work at the Scottish women's hospital in Salonika. By the end of 1916 the slight decline in the number of female arts students was attributed to women leaving for war work. The graduates established a women's war register listing the qualifications and experience of women available to fill professional, commercial or industrial posts to free men for military service,[50] and several women graduates were appointed to the Intelligence Department of the War Office.

Volunteers from the university served free refreshments to service men at the rest room on Aberdeen railway station. As the war progressed students noticed the increasing reluctance of servicemen to discuss their experiences, but the voluntary work was not always gloomy; a graduate remembered cheerful times spent there and recalled the occasion one woman put a dirty hand into the churn of butter which promptly turned grey. By 1916 the *materia medica* department had been invaded by sewing machines and Robert Gordon's College and Aberdeen University had become major centres for the sorting of sphagnum moss which was subsequently sent to all parts of the war arena. There were frequent calls for more volunteers for the War Work Party, but there were few women who were not already involved, and during summer vacations war work continued on the farms. There were student graduates 'to whom peasemeal fights and torchlight processions are an idle tale! . . . Professors have come and professors have gone . . . and the world of lecturers and assistants has been turned topsy-turvey'.[51] One symptom of the upheaval was the number of women employed in such posts: by 1916 there were eight female assistants in the university.

All the women students lost class-mates; many also suffered family bereavements. As the war continued, those who remained discussed the ethics of their own position and debated whether there should be conscription for women in war-time and equal sacrifice for all. Most of them accepted the view of the authorities that their training would be urgently needed after the war. *Alma Mater* considered the future of female medical graduates: 'The need for trained and educated women will perhaps never have been so great. . . . We believe there is a big future for women workers in infant welfare, school inspection and like forms of work, as well as in general practice'.[52]

By the end of the first year of the war students were also questioning the ethics of participating in student activities whilst their class-mates were being killed. However, the decision to suspend the Women's Debating Society in 1915 was criticised on the grounds that those who had died had seen university life as an all-round environment, including societies and other social activities, and this tradition should be continued—especially by the women who were in a better position to do so.[53] Meetings of the WDS were resumed for a few months, but too many other matters intruded, and the society's activities were again suspended. Nevertheless, whilst the most influential positions in student-organised activities, such as control of the SRC, remained in the hands of a small caucus of male students, particularly senior medics who were in any case generally older than other students, many other posts were filled by women, including the sub-editorship and in 1917–18 the editorship of *Alma Mater*.

The men's debating society had collapsed in 1913. Subsequently, a subcommittee of the Union, consisting of the president and six more members, plus the presidents of the Agricultural, Celtic, Medical, Literary, Scientific and Sociological societies, was formed to organise university debates. By the 1916–17 session the presidents of the last three societies were all women, so war-time debates were organised as well as attended by both male and female students. This precipitated the formation of a mixed-sex debating society after the war, though when the University Debating Society was initially restarted it indicated every intention of continuing where it had left off, with the proposal that only matriculated male students should be eligible for membership. This was out-voted and at the beginning of the next session the society tested its new look with the provocative proposition 'that women are a wet blanket in any society'. The leading arguments brought forward had not changed, even after a quarter of a century of female university students and the trauma of the Great War, but there were differences: the speakers included two women, the negative won by a large majority, it was voted to admit women to full membership of the society and women were elected onto the committee.[54]

Meanwhile, as the war dragged on and the list of dead and injured grew there was a reaction to the horror by some students and the number of social functions began to increase again. There was also friction amongst student groups, particularly the male and female medical students who became involved in some acrimonious correspondence. But regardless of criticism, or possibly the underlying cause, female students in general were becoming more aware of themselves and of changes in their own attitudes and confidence. The women's issue of *Alma Mater* contrasted the girl of 1914 with that of 1915: 'And yet, if it is not reflected without it is more certain that there has been a revolution within'.[55]

The new note of self-confidence was evident in mildly unconventional behaviour by the women, such as swearing, kicking stones in the street, sliding down the banisters or riding a motorbike,[56] as well as in discussions in which the subject matter embraced a range of feminine interests rather than suffrage alone. The Sociological Society heard papers relating the suffrage question to the feminist movement and examining why women's wages were lower than men's. The women's debating society discussed whether women would be retained in industry when the war was over and heard that women students had not been effectively portrayed in literature. The Science Society heard a paper on pioneering women in science, the Women's Medical Society a paper on pioneering women medics and on future opportunities.[57] After the war a short-lived but energetic women's political society considered such matters as the effect of legislation on women, women's wages, income tax from women's point of view, aspects of the current social unrest, the National Council of Women, and housing: 'All barriers have been swept aside, and it remains with us to show ourselves worthy of the opportunities these pioneers have made possibile to us'.[58] *Alma Mater*'s woman editor suggested:

> that at present intelligence is on the whole a monopoly of the women students . . . how many [male] students are there who have thought seriously on such things as education and industrial reconstruction, state control of health and the enfranchisement of women? These are not questions for airy speculation, but matters of practical concern for the community.[59]

Along with this increased self-confidence, some of the women became more assertive. Mary Sutherland, who was to become the Chief Woman Officer of the Labour Party, told the Sociological Society that two specific manifestations of socialism were:

> the new interest in education and the women's movement. The real justification of the latter is the fact that it aims at altering a system which depends on the subordination of the human element to the sex element, for it is coming to be realised that in most of life the question of sex is irrelevant and opportunities should be equal for men and women alike.[60]

Two weeks after women over thirty were given the vote the women's number of *Alma Mater* took stock of women's position and looked forward to the post-war period:

> It is curiously significant that the issue of the fourth women's number since the beginning of the war finds us still debating the question of the place of women in the Universities. That question, for some of us, was decided long ago; the answer to it was implicit from the very moment that women were admitted to the Universities; it became a matter of time and patience and detail . . .
>
> The question of the place of women in the University or in any one Faculty of it is merely a particular aspect of the wider problem of the position of women in modern society. . . . Both in the University and out of it women have proved themselves efficient and capable members of the community. As a general rule the war has only helped to accelerate the pace of change that was coming over the whole of social life. Men and women are fellow-workers first, and men and women second . . .
>
> The great social work of the century on which we have little more than entered, would seem to be the securing of the practical means towards equality of opportunity for the education and work of women in common with all other members of the community.[61]

In 1919 Ordinance 18 (General no. 9) admitting women to the Scottish universities was repealed; following the passing of Section 3 of the Sex Discrimination Act it was no longer necessary.

Chapter 8

Gender Relations

Students or ladies?

Isabella Asher, one of the first women students, described the initial response to their presence:

> Such courtesy we received! Would we sit in the back or the front benches, the professors asked. We were invited to all the Cinderellas and asked to sit on the committees of the various societies. When any of us scored well in the class tests there were rounds of generous applause. I well remember in the Logic classroom on the day before we broke up for the Christmas vacation, four little dolls, four little bags of sweets and four musical tops were laid on the desk in front of us.[1]

In 1906 Mary Ramsay commented that:

> the politeness shown by the men has been invariable and universal; the unwritten laws of etiquette which rule in the relation between the men and the women are excellent in character, and have contributed to maintain the high tone of University life, the *esprit de corps*, and the pride that both the sexes take in their University.[2]

A third-year arts student attending at the beginning of the century concurred that she had 'never yet met a male student who did not know how to treat a lady'.[3] Other personal reminiscences, even of those who attended the university later when women students had lost their curiosity value and relations between the sexes were not always so harmonious, were in a similar vein.

There was a subtle but clear distinction between this type of personal relationship and general expressions of opinion about the social roles of, or biological differences between, the sexes, when the most insulting remarks could be made about women in the abstract without social etiquette being breached. But anyone who crossed the dividing line was quickly reprimanded. In 1911 the Debating Society minutes recorded that one student's speech had been 'full of improper allusions. This speaker was not a success; and in the presence of a large company of ladies he cannot be said to have helped the reputation of the Debating Society'. On another occasion the SRC supported a complaint that descriptions of personalities in an issue of *Alma Mater* went beyond 'the bounds of ordinary propriety in so far as they concern *lady* students'.[4]

In both personal relationships and abstract debates, the differences between the sexes were clearly demarcated. But there were situations when the emphasis was on behaviour seen as characteristic of 'students' rather than gender-specific; and it was here that there was often the greatest ambiguity since student traditions had originated in a male culture and it was not always certain whether a woman could behave as a typical 'student' and yet still remain a 'lady'. The women adopted the 'student' ethos about lodgings, for example, but were less inclined to contravene the social conventions governing femininity by taking an active part in student societies. Such ambiguous signals left male students uncertain how they should interact with the women:

> When we began to attend classes at King's we entered into a new world. We had come up from the town and country schools, and I am sure the idea of a 'co-ed' college had never occurred to us. So when we found lady students sitting on the same benches as ourselves and listening to the same lectures, we had to adjust ourselves to quite a new situation. The reactions were various. How would this affect the professions? How would it affect the ladies themselves? Would they be able to compete on equal terms with men? These questions were constantly discussed during our undergraduate days and *Alma Mater* was full of references to them.
>
> I think the underlying doubt beneath all this discussion was whether the ladies could play their part in university life, since that life had modelled itself through the ages according to the supposed needs and capacities of men.[5]

There was discussion as to whether being a member of the same class counted as an 'introduction' or whether members of the opposite sex should wait to be formally introduced before addressing each other. One writer argued that 'men and women, on becoming members of a university, where they are legally and officially on the same footing, cease to be men and women differentiated as such; they become instead members of a corporate body—the undergraduates of the university', but a respondent argued that a formal introduction was considered necessary between men and women in all polite society and there was no reason why universities should be any different.[6]

There was the question of what to call female students and how, indeed, they should describe themselves. The professors were usually formal, though at least one called women as well as men by surname only. At first *Alma Mater* referred archly to the 'lady students', the term formally adopted by the Senatus; but soon feminine versions of the men's year names were in use for the first three arts years—bajanella, semilina and tertiana—though a feminine equivalent of the fourth-year 'magistrand' was seldom applied and the medical versions—lambella and clementine— were less often used.

Another issue was whether women should wear hats in classes. It was a little while before those in the first English classes acted, but soon 'hats off' became the rule at Aberdeen. The symbolic importance of this gesture (apart from its pragmatic convenience) was not missed by a French student visiting in 1905: 'The first difference which I remarked is that Scotch girls put off their hats to attend lectures. And this practice has appeared to me a sign of real brotherhood and work between male and female students'.[7] A related question was whether women students should wear feminine clothes or student garb, an issue which was complicated by the fact that the scarlet gown and trencher were not invariably worn by all male students, though the SRC and *Alma Mater* pressed the issue in an attempt to promote a corporate student identity.[8] The women did wear the gown, but at first modified the sleeves to fit conveniently over dresses and differentiated themselves from the men by having a scarlet rather than black tassel on their trenchers, an innovation greeted with delighted horror on its debut, though even this distinction was criticised by one student as a germ 'from which, if nourished, there will spring an entire separation between the men and women of the university'.[9] The issue of dress reached its high point in 1902 when the SRC persuaded the women students 'not without a little difficulty' to attend the annual student night at the theatre wearing academic costume rather than (or presumably over) their evening dress. A committee was formed amongst the women students to organise this and the SRC expressed themselves delighted with the result—'their display in the Dress Circle was well worth witnessing'. The following year women students were requested to wear academic costume for the rectorial address too and in later years the women students were more assiduous about wearing the gown for lectures than their male colleagues.[10]

Horseplay, which degenerated into drunken hooliganism on ritual occasions, was considered an integral part of the male university ethos, epitomised by activities such as snowball fights, pushing and shoving on the stairs, the tearing of new students' gowns and the 'peasemeal fight' at rectorial elections.[11] Women did not participate but their approval was considered important. At Strathcona's rectorial address:

THE ACADEMIC WOMAN.

"Lay not the flattering unction to thy heart."
Hamlet.

First old Woman (overheard in the Spital)—Fat are ye makin' o' *your* dother?

Second old Woman (airily)—Nae a pupil-teacher, noo. Na—my man was readin' in the bit pepper they ca' *Alma Mater*, that fifty per cent o' the weemin that gaed to the medicals, either get scunnert or get marriet—so, ye see, the craitur' micht "haud-in a back chap," and get a man that wye?

First old Woman (dubiously)—Imphm!

I.

In other days, when learning rose
They founded colleges for *men*:
A nation leaders found in those—
Their maker's image,—with a brain—
Then Scotland flourished, and her name
At least could court the open glare
Of criticism, and her fame
For learning flourished everywhere:
Now falls her hopes on other days,
On evil tongues, and evil ways.

II.

Domestic servants now are few,
And far between the L.L.A.'s;
But glut the market, and the new
Fad now is all to be M.A.'s,
Or even librarians is the craze:
Their mothers—better women—took
Their *ma*-degrees by wiser ways
Than always grinding in a book.
The world was better guided then,
And would be if 'twere so again.

III.

Tinned-meats and penny cookery books,
With white-seam done but once a week!
"These be thy gods, O Israel!"—cooks
Like these alack, are sore to seek;
They furnish but a sorry freak
To any man that wants a wife,
Even Moses self had not been meek
With such a partner for his life:—
The best of woman will *not* roam
As Bajans, but are found at home.

VIRTUTE CRESCO.

17 *AM*, 12 (1894–5), p 35.

THE LADY BAJAN'S REPLY TO VIRTUTE CRESCO.

Home keeping youth hath ever homely wits.
—*Shakespeare.*

O nameless censor that would pass
  A judgment on our head and heart !
Thou grow'st in valour, but alas—
  Thou know'st not valour's better part.
Forego thy wistful prophecies
  Of a lost culinary art :—
We pray thee of thy courtesy
  To let the Lady Bajans be.

Shall we, who tread the devious paths
  That scale the crags of the degree—
The ways of Latin, Greek, and Maths.,
  With all its woeful gramarye,
Fail at a dinner's mysteries,
  When Love is Prof. and Love is Fee ?
We pray thee of thy courtesy
  To let the Lady Bajans be.

The prince of whom OUR souls do dream,
  Moreover, stands a man complete ;
HE doth not sensuously deem
  Humanity doth " live to eat."
He knows divine philosophies,
  Nor weighs the woes of " tinnéd meat."
We *would* not wed with thine or thee,
  Oh ! let the Lady Bajan's be.

We shall not give an empty brain
  To him who takes the love that's life,
Our daughters' daughters yet shall reign
  As perfect woman, perfect wife.
But kitchen damsels, since they please
  Thy palate better, still are rife :—
Meanwhile we sweep a courtesy,
  And leave thee in thy gluttony.
  Oh ! let the Lady Bajans be !

A LADY BAJAN.

18 *AM*, 12 (1894–5), p 45.

> one or two [male students] were literally passed up to the gallery, whence the sympathetic arms of the ladies were stretched out to save them from falling, and to help them into the gallery. Some of the pieces of woodwork were damaged . . . nobody was hurt and all enjoyed the fun – the lady students as much as anyone else.[12]

A woman who defended the behaviour of the male students at the 1903 rectorial was herself praised by another student and the SRC was pleased when women offered to help raise funds to cover the cost of the carriage smashed during the 1909 rectorial.[13]

When women students were more actively involved, *Alma Mater* acted as unofficial arbiter, simultaneously reporting behaviour felt to border on the edge of what was permissible for relationships between the sexes and approving women's acceptance of such behaviour. Male members of the first mixed English class were chided for pulling the ladies' hair and generally annoying them, and a student who tossed off a woman's hat during a lecture might find the incident publicly recorded. The women in one of the French classes were reported as protesting bitterly 'against the conduct of a certain youthful individual who comes to lectures provided with a squirt. They say that what troubles them most is that they have never been assured that the water is clean'.[14] Outsiders were especially horrified by the ribaldry and shouts women had to face at the notoriously uncouth graduation ceremonies.[15] Mild fun between women, such as one knocking the pen from another's ear, was more approved of than the unstudent-like activity of walking with their arms entwined around each other; but as the response to suffrage activities indicated, the permissible limits of such behaviour were sharply drawn.

Nevertheless, women such as those who objected to the 'ungentlemanly' behaviour of the male students who threw snowballs at them in the Quad had no doubts as to whether they were first and foremost 'ladies' or 'students', and very pompous they could be on the subject:

> Would any of your correspondents be so kind as to explain why ladies are charged for going to see the matches played on King's College Grounds? Surely this is a startling innovation. There are few, if any, grounds in this country where ladies are charged, and it is certainly not worthy of Aberdeen University. It is a shock to a lady after walking through the gate calmly to be called back and asked for her sixpence like an ordinary man.[16]

One of the main elements of the existing student ethos was 'the class'. Previously students matriculating in any one year had all moved systematically through the same courses and inevitably a bond formed between many of the class members, which was strengthened by year names, class suppers, reunions, and the maintenance of class records after graduation. The change of the university curriculum under the 1889 Commissioners signalled the unavoidable dissolution of this bond because of the introduction of a wide variety of course options, but the inevitable change was stoutly resisted by the traditionalists and for the next ten or fifteen years there was perhaps a more self-conscious effort to promote the class *esprit de corps* than before.

One situation where it was necessary for both male and female students to decide whether the women were to be considered primarily as fellow students or as ladies was over the question of class suppers. In 1892 the bajanellas were invited to attend the first-year supper but were too timid to accept. The debate in *Alma Mater* in subsequent years reflected the ambiguity felt by the traditionalists, torn between promoting the corporate class spirit, yet not wishing to alter the format of these drinking and smoking occasions which were seen as a part of the university tradition on a par with the Choral Society.[17] As the number of female students increased so did the hostility of the men towards the idea of changing their behaviour and therefore their tradition for the benefit of the women, yet the deliberate exclusion of what might be half, or more, of a class on an occasion intended to promote its social unity was clearly hypocritical. The issue was debated afresh each year and in 1905 the first year students voted for an 'At Home' rather than a class supper, the third-year students of the previous year having been the first to hold a class dance. The following year the new students held both a social evening and an all-male class supper and this was repeated on a number of occasions before the class dance finally replaced the class supper. In 1907, when a student suggested that the third-year supper should be teetotal so that women could attend, a woman commented that his chivalry 'ought to bring a blush to the cheeks of his brutal, bubulous, selfish and uncivilised seniors'. But the tertianas had 'received too many hints hitherto that our presence in the Varsity has put a stop to these worthy Bacchanalian orgies—that we are decidedly *de trop*'. They therefore organised their own supper, 'a social evening with tea, vocal and instrumental selections and speeches, political and academic, and one or two things entirely new generously offered by some of the ladies'.[18] The activities of the 1908–12 class illustrated the influence of the women students and the new emphasis on a greater variety of social activities.[19] In the first year there were two At Homes at Kennaway's Cafe and a picnic excursion; in the second year class dances and another picnic were arranged as well as a class supper for the male students, and in the third year the women held a social evening and the men a class supper; the year after graduation the class held a reunion dance in Kennaway's Rooms, followed the next day by an afternoon gathering in the West End Cafe for the women and a class dinner for the men.

Similar uncertainty about the advantage of considering women part of the corporate entity existed in connection with student societies. Officially women's membership was seen as something to be encouraged,[20] yet equivocation was evident in the response of both male and female students—if women were students then they should be participating more actively; if they were 'ladies', then some discussions or activities were not suitable for mixed groups and separate societies were preferable.[21] Whilst societies such as the Celtic, Modern Languages or the Tennis Club which started as single-sex became mixed, others such as the Christian Union reversed the trend, as students found it difficult to discuss moral issues in mixed company. Although, as Anderson has shown, the growth of student societies, sporting clubs and cultural activities originated in the 1880s from the movement to develop a student 'corporate ideal',[22] women were often considered responsible for the proliferation of such social activities by those who were less enthusiastic about this development. Nor was the increasing popularity of class and society At Homes and dances viewed with universal approval.

The extent of women's assimilation into the student culture could be measured by their involvement in the 1906 quatercentenary celebrations. Much of this was in the form of separate activities. The all-male SRC organised sports, a torchlight procession and 'smokers'. The female students formed their own committee to organise activities; they walked separately in the big procession, they hosted women delegates to a separate supper in the Union followed by music, and they held an At Home at Robert Gordon's College. But mixed activities were also arranged, including a Choral Society presentation, a student ball and a tableaux at the theatre.

Attitudes towards women students

Views about women reflected in the debate about their admission to higher education in the 1870s and 1880s did not simply disappear the moment women were admitted to the university. Both male and female students and the teaching staff brought their prejudices and expectations with them, and since the university was predominantly a male institution, it was men's views which were preponderant. As one of them recalled: 'The attitude of the average male in those days was one of humorous tolerance imposed upon the underlying conviction of male superiority'.[23] This betrayed an assumption of male intellectual superiority[24] and a belief that women were unfitted for public activities such as politics, administration or professional occupations.[25]

Various methods were used to reinforce the message of women's true character and natural inferiority, including student debates, class supper speeches and dramatic farces, but the most potent was the student magazine. *Alma Mater* had started in 1883, becoming the official organ of the students under the control of the newly established SRC in 1888. The paper, which appeared every week during term, and generally also ran some summer issues, carried student news intermingled with some serious articles by both students and graduates and occasional biographies or examination results, all packaged in a series of in-jokes. Women were encouraged to contribute, but faced with the *de facto* male editorial control were slow to do so. The first article by a female student appeared in 1896 and one or two women were appointed to the editorial board from 1897 onwards. A column for women students started in 1898 and the first women's issue appeared in 1910, but the first female editor was not elected until 1913, when Agnes Mure Mackenzie edited the summer issues. Despite the nominal nod in the women's direction, the paper remained firmly under the control of the male Union/SRC clique and until the First World War the paper was essentially 'edited by men for men'.

Male students who were strongly opposed to the presence of women students, especially older graduates who were more remote from everyday student life and less reconciled to the changes, often wrote with considerable hostility about student women. Others were shyer about outright criticism and often camouflaged their argument in verse, which appeared in considerable quantities and varying quality at moments of controversy such as the appearance of the first female students or the antagonism caused by the women's efforts to gain SRC representation. Only occasionally did women respond in kind.

A subtle but important difference during the war period was the absence of the subliminal reinforcement of chauvinistic views which had been evident for the first thirty years of *Alma Mater*. Previously every issue had carried jokes and innuendo at the expense of women and articles or dialogues on topics such as why to remain single, the landlady or the mother-in-law. Women students (in the abstract) were represented as silly, uninterested in academic or intellectual matters, and concerned only with men, marriage, clothes, hats, fashion and gossip.[26] The implication was always that this was woman's nature and could not be altered—it was 'characteristic of women to be narrow and prejudiced in their views'; 'a silent woman is either a genius or an absolute idiot, and in any case is an abnormality, a freak of nature'; 'a woman never reasons, she concludes'; 'the flow of language at women's command [is] in direct proportion to the insignificance of the topic'.[27] Such remarks were always present, making their impression like the constant drip of water, the more damaging for the absence of any malicious intent on the part of the writers. Occasionally they were inspired. Having dealt in pithy fashion with the behaviour of the male students in a certain class, the writer turned to the women members: 'from the none too subdued murmur ascending from the back benches, one would almost suppose that by some anatomical variation the tongues of ladies were slung in the middle and wagged at both ends'.[28]

Sometimes women's 'natural' attributes could be put to useful purpose. Writing of the forthcoming quatercentenary celebrations a male student commented that:

> even the lady students—often a neglected factor in University life—are to have enough to keep them busy. There are a thousand and one little things that tasteful femininity will be called upon to do, and we are confident that there will be no lack of busy fingers and busier brains to do them.[29]

However, the women were warned not to presume that the fact that their advice had been sought in connection with the quatercentenary decorations meant that it 'would be equally welcome or valuable in more important matters'.[30] Sewing and decoration were women's work; organisation and administration were not.

Any woman whose behaviour did not measure up to the expected standard was liable to attack, sometimes directly, but more often again through ridicule or sarcasm. The first women students were examples of the 'new woman'. Those who actively campaigned for political power, either in the university or the country at large from 1907 were described as 'mannish women'. The new woman was intellectual and undomesticated, smoked and rode a bicycle. The mannish woman was demanding, loud-mouthed, capable of public repartee and physical violence. As in more recent attacks on feminism, women's critics argued that women who campaigned for independence and power were not truly feminine and therefore not entitled to the respect accorded to a lady. 'It is to those man-women, crosses between fanaticism and madness, that the SRC has had to grant this new clause', a student wrote, referring to the allocation of five council seats to female students.[31] Man's character was of course the norm and as such too obvious to be described, but one writer commented that whilst deploring masculine women, a woman who could 'lay claim to some of man's virtues such as independence of thought, pluck and commonsense' was much to be preferred to the old-fashioned sort.[32]

Complaints were sometimes made that the presence of women adversely affected the men's academic standards, either because of women's intellectual inferiority or because of their disturbing sensuality.[33] In 1913 Keith Leask, an ex-Aberdeen student and assistant and the most persistent of the anti-women campaigners, referred contemptuously to the students cramming for a pass degree—mostly women aiming at the teaching profession—who studied from purely utilitarian motives and had no great ability or wider or deeper intellectual curiosity. He disparagingly contrasted these students with those of his own student days. But John Bulloch, recalling that the most heavily used library resources in his pre-women student days had not been the books but the old examination papers, likened the university of the 1880s to a factory mechanically stuffing turkeys for Christmas and considered the old all-male system had produced many mediocre and immature men.[34] Others quoted the prize lists as proof that women students had shown themselves capable of competing with the men and it was argued that as they were generally harder working their presence actually helped raise standards because men disliked being beaten by them.[35] On the other hand, the fall in the average age of women students changed the relationship between male and female students and encouraged the growth of that 'amatory disquietude' which, as Bulloch observed, 'plays ducks and drakes with work'.[36]

There was more force to the opposition's criticisms in the case of medicine, the class situation in which the student/gender dichotomy was felt most sharply. At the turn of the century male students voiced the embarrassment they felt at discussing certain cases, especially those dealing with sexual diseases, before mixed audiences. The female student numbers did not warrant separation and the Royal Infirmary was not large enough for wards to be set aside for them, so it was argued that the presence of women would curtail (or was curtailing) the teaching the male students obtained.[37] When it was suggested it would be preferable if intending female candidates went to cities where separate medical schools for women were available, thus solving the problem for everyone, the women students responded that they wished to 'be regarded—or disregarded as fellow students' rather than as ladies.[38] The number of women attending medical classes was so small during the pre-war years that the issue remained quiescent, although as earlier events at Edinburgh had illustrated, any number could be sufficient to make an issue of the matter if the male students and staff felt strongly enough. Professor Hay told the 1909 Committee on Scottish Universities:

> Of course, sometimes one hears the men students talk as if they did not care much about women attending classes alongside of them, but it has never come to much in Aberdeen. No formal complaint has been submitted to the University Court or even to the Senatus, and I do not think the complaint is even much voiced in the students' special paper *Alma Mater*. On the whole they get on very well together.[39]

But from a nadir of six matriculated women medical students in 1906, their number rose to eighteen in 1912–13 and then increased rapidly during the war, rising to 124 by 1917–18. Combined with the drop in the number of male students this meant that during the 1916–17 and 1917–18 sessions women students constituted over a third of the medical faculty. The speed with which this unprecedented situation developed not unnaturally resulted in friction. There were references to antagonisms between the sexes and between the older and younger students, and some of the female students complained of unfair treatment.[40] Now it was the medical men's turn to complain they were being reduced to effeminacy and to argue that because the women were less able and their presence was distracting, they prevented men from producing their best work.[41] The student/gender ambiguity resurfaced. One article in *Alma Mater* illustrated especially clearly the extent to which men blamed their own reaction to the presence of women students on the women themselves. The writer complained that the women medics demanded equal rights and privileges with the male students, but also expected to be treated preferentially as women. Women might *say* they did not want to be treated as women, he continued, but whatever his scientific training no man could ever regard a woman in any other light.[42] Some of the women again objected to the insinuation that they expected different or preferential treatment: 'As Women Medicals, we have long been aware of the hostility to our presence and have even acquired a certain degree of immunity to it, but the charge brought against us in the last *Alma Mater* is a much more serious one'. They argued that women gave up much to take up medicine and only did so because they were strongly motivated and wanted to work alongside men; not as a separate group and certainly not as rivals.[43]

The lower entrance examination set for medical students meant that students could matriculate younger than for the arts degree and many of the newly recruited war-time girls had come straight from school at the age of seventeen or even sixteen. Whilst understandable anxiety was expressed by the older women about the maturity of such girls to cope with the personal and social demands of medical practice,[44] some of the male students reverted to casting aspersions on women's motives for entering university,[45] a response criticised by several women; as one commented, their motives were as varied as the men's and no less worthy.[46]

Occasionally, male grumbles erupted into demands for segregation within student societies, the medical faculty, or even the whole university, as in 1909 when the issue was raised throughout Scotland by a vote for separate universities at the SRC inter-university conference,[47] and again in 1911 when Leask tried to rouse the male students to positive action against the presence of women:

> At present the numbers are temporarily kept up by the female infusion, that deadliest blow to the Higher Learning of poor old Scotland. . . . Is it not notorious, proclaimed everywhere, that the University societies have become absolutely worthless? That some classes have attracted the females in such numbers as to be useless to the men who contemptuously boycott them. . . . Are not the graduates all over the North very plain in their declaration that the *whole mental tone* of the University has been altered and degraded, and that 'cinder-men' and 'Kennaway' women have devastated the old manly atmosphere by the introduction of the pestilential miasma of a flabby hermaphroditism? . . . Universities exist for Higher Learning only, not for females. If the men are not to miss 'their place in the sun' they must speak out and let it be very clearly known and seen that Bajanellas and the great traditions of King's College can not and shall not be conjoined. The place for the first is elsewhere—outside.[48]

Leask's attempt was unsuccessful. Only one correspondent wrote agreeing that it was 'a distraction and a disgrace' to have men and women attending the same university. Adam, an ex-editor, ably defended the women from an 'extraordinary (and very nearly insulting) diatribe'.[49]

The lack of excitement amongst male Aberdeen students about the admission of women contrasted with events at Cambridge in 1896 and 1897 when a debate was attended by over one thousand students and a petition asking the Senate to keep women out of the university was signed by two thousand, while their riotous behaviour on the day of the vote in 1919 was to become famous. By comparison even the fifty Aberdeen students who rampaged during the 1908 women's suffrage meeting were a tiny minority. The idea that student views should be taken into consideration was an alien concept in the English universities but as the Cambridge experience showed, university professors and graduates were not above using it when suited them. Nearer to home, the Edinburgh University Court referred to petitions from its SRC and male medical students as a reason for refusing to admit women to its medical classes in 1909.[50] The Aberdeen students, like those of the other Scottish universities, had been granted official participation in the control of the university; the rector and rector's assessor were theoretically the students' representatives on the University Court and the SRC was officially recognised by the 1889 Universities (Scotland) Act. So although Aberdeen student numbers were small, they could expect to be heeded and, indeed, they had proved in the past that they could force the authorities to take action if they felt strongly enough about a matter.[51] But only a minority of male students took student politics or university traditions so seriously. For the majority, their assumption of male superiority and their humorous tolerance of the women students was manifested in a combination of gentlemanly chivalry, male chauvinism and student comradeship. The most common response of those who disliked the presence of women was one of resignation; it would have been better for men and women to have separate colleges, but the decision had been made and the misogynists would have to accept it.[52] Most students got on with their work and made little fuss. Moreover, many of the men had sisters, or had friends who had sisters at Aberdeen; a quarter of the women students graduating between 1901 and 1921 had at least one brother who also graduated from the university and other male students came up from co-educational schools and already knew some of the women students, while 9 per cent of those graduating between 1901 and 1925 subsequently married a female colleague.[53] In 1907 the men's debating society voted in favour of mixed colleges; as a woman who matriculated that year remarked, most of the men enjoyed the presence of women[54] and a considerable proportion also approved of the changes in university life. Adam commented:

> It is very true that the influx of women to our University has altered the *whole mental tone*—perhaps some of us in all seriousness, thank God for that. That wonderful 'old manly atmosphere' looks very bright and clear from a distance of thirty years, but . . . the students of long ago had their full share of hard coarse living. Ethics aside, I believe we can mark a clear advance in culture . . . We are, I firmly maintain, just as capable of the strongest and finest feelings as were the students of Mr Leask's day and we are certainly a little more polite about it. 'Kennaway women' and 'Cinder-men' are among our best types of students—they are men and women capable not only of taking their place in all educational circles, but capable also of appearing to advantage in the much wider and more important circle of the cultured world.[55]

Analysis of student reactions has concentrated on the attitude of the male majority, but throughout the period a third or more of the Aberdeen men supported even the most radical developments of the women's movement. In 1892 Bulloch had perceptively summarised the long-term consequences of admitting women to the university in words which aptly explained why so many nineteenth-century feminists had devoted so much effort to obtaining higher education for women:

> 'I think,' says Nora Helmer in *A Doll's House*, 'that before all else I am a human being. Henceforth I can't be satisfied with what most people say, and what is in books. I must think things out for myself, and try to get clear about them.' It is hard for every man to say amen. It is forgotten that, with the same education as men, women will, within certain limits, possess the same aspirations as men. A woman better equipped at the start than her antiquated sisters cannot be expected to sink into the rut they have been accustomed to follow. That rut has been one walled in by the theory and

ON THIN ICE

19 *AM*, 13 (1895–6), p 94.

practice of man's infinite superiority; and this has raised the barrier of patronage—euphemised as 'gallantry'—which must stultify any acquirements that would put the sexes on some sort of equal footing. The dim perception of what the new movement means is not reserved for men. It seems almost certain that when higher education for women has passed from being an amusement, and when the novelty has worn off, women must be prepared to be treated in a way quite different to what they have received in past. The whole of our social relations with women is based on the primary assumption of their weakness. When, by successful competition with men that has been proved to be a fallacy, the social code is bound to be modified, if not altogether changed and a relationship similar to what exists between man and man will take its place. This is a contingency for which many advanced women are not prepared, but it is merely the logical conclusion of the movement now at work. It need not be a terrifying prospect except to the bigots of both sexes who juggle with such abstractions as 'womanliness' or 'blue stocking'. We, in Aberdeen, are just on the first rung of the ladder. No one need complain of the monotony of our academic system when such a problem is being worked out before our eyes.[56]

Chapter 9

Occupational and Social Mobility

Social origins of female students

Women students at Aberdeen between 1894 and 1920 were overwhelmingly local; over 60 per cent of the arts women matriculating in 1908 were born in the five counties of north-east Scotland and the figure had increased to 71 per cent by 1924. Most of the remainder came from the Highlands or the north of Scotland and only a few—3 per cent in 1908 and 6.7 per cent in 1924—were born outside Scotland. Non-arts women were slightly less local.[1]

A quarter of the women came from professional families; the churches and education were the two largest categories, though the proportion of ministers' daughters declined during the period under review. Some of them came from very poor families; the daughter of a rural Aberdeenshire minister with nine children recalled that her father had never had an annual income of more than £120.[2] Fathers in education (who formed a surprisingly small proportion of the parents of female students) ranged from HMIs and university professors to the teachers of small rural schools.

Few women whose fathers were manufacturing owners or managers attended the university. Commerce was better represented, but largely on the merchant rather than the financial side. Merchants ranged from those with large businesses in the city to rural suppliers more akin to lower middle-class members such as traders and shopkeepers. Though minor officials and clerks were also represented, it was tradesmen who formed the bulk of the fathers of lower middle-class women graduates.

One-fifth of the women students at Aberdeen between 1894 and 1920 came from farming families. The cultural and economic environment of these students is difficult to summarise because this occupation covered a wide range, but did not carry the high social status awarded to professionals by their own community. Farmers could be extremely wealthy men with large properties, whose life-styles were close to those of manufacturing owners or large merchants, and who sent their daughters to private schools in the city or away to Edinburgh. But at the other end of the scale were small farmers or crofters who were little more than subsistence farmers, helped by all the family and drifting at times into other occupations to subsidise their income.

Women from working class families more often came from local rural areas, reflecting the traditional rapport between some of the rural schools and the university, especially when, as at Strichen and Fordyce, there were school and university bursaries available. Of a sample of seventy-three working-class women graduates who sat the bursary competition, 8 per cent came from Aberdeen city and 78 per cent from the North East. Of a sample of twenty-nine women from working-class backgrounds who did not sit the examination, 34 per cent came from Aberdeen city and 52 per cent from the North East.[3]

A comparison of women students who completed a full course compared with those who attended in only one or two subjects shows a considerable bias in the early years.[4]

TABLE 7 CLASS ATTENDANCE BY WOMEN ARTS STUDENTS, MATRICULATING 1898 AND 1901, CLASSIFIED BY FATHER'S OCCUPATION (PERCENTAGES).

	1898		1901	
Occupation	*Full course*	*Selected classes*	*Full course*	*Selected classes*
Indep. means	—	—	—	3.2
Professional	40.0	13.0	26.9	9.7
Commerce	6.7	8.7	19.2	—
Industry	13.3	—	—	3.2
Agriculture	—	—	11.5	32.3
Tradesmen etc.	6.7	34.8	19.2	12.9
Working-class				
(Skilled)	6.7	17.4	3.8	16.1
(Unskilled)	6.7	13.0	3.8	6.5
Not known	20.0	13.0	15.4	16.1
Total	100.1	99.9	99.8	100
Numbers	15	23	26	31

This was an indication of the larger number of lower middle-class and working-class student teachers who were funded by the SED for only one or two years, or only able to qualify for attendance in one or two subjects. That most student teachers were women was reflected in the fact that

12 per cent of the men but 27 per cent of the women who matriculated in 1903 attended for only one year.[5] Their numbers were not balanced by the small number of private students from wealthier families, who took only one or two subjects or attended for only a year or so preparatory to admission elsewhere. A comparison of graduation and matriculation over the longer period 1900–10 (table 8) is made difficult by the large number of 'unknowns' in one sample, but in essence variation in the graduation rate of women students by social class declined, though working-class entrants were still under-represented. An increase in the proportion of working-class graduates was the most notable feature of the years 1911–1920, though access to the university was of course heavily weighted by social class.

Access to higher education

The difference in the social class composition of those attending Aberdeen compared with those at the elite women's colleges in England was due to the relatively low cost of attendance and the greater availability of financial assistance and free or cheap secondary education.

Few students living away from home managed as frugally as those in Aberdeen. In 1902 it was estimated that an Aberdeen student would need £25 for board and lodging to attend both the winter and summer sessions without returning home (a period of thirty-eight weeks), plus £10 to cover fees, books and subscriptions to societies, and additional money for clothes and travelling expenses.[6] Until 1909 the summer session was optional for arts students except those studying for the honours degree or attending as King's Students, and those who could not afford even this expense attended only the winter session which might be managed for a total outlay of about £30. By 1913 lodgings cost between 12*s*. and 23*s*. 6*d*. and the price rose more sharply after the war, but even in 1920, at between 30*s*. and 35*s*. a week, they were reported to be amongst the cheapest available in Britain.[7]

Few substantial scholarships were available at Aberdeen and none were provided specifically for women students, but students were likely to obtain at least some financial assistance from one of three sources. From 1901 to 1910 the Carnegie Trust paid the entire fee of Scottish students, though in 1906–7 when the arts fee was raised from three to four guineas per subject the Trust introduced tighter requirements. From 1911 onwards only part of the cost of the fees was paid because of the growth in student numbers. There was no means test, but students had to have spent two years in a Scottish school. In 1910, 90 per cent of the women at Aberdeen had their fees (averaging £10. 5*s*. for a year's course) paid by the

TABLE 8 FATHER'S OCCUPATION OF ABERDEEN WOMEN STUDENTS 1900–10, AND ABERDEEN WOMEN GRADUATES 1898–1920 (PERCENTAGES).[8]

Matriculating:	*1900–10*	*(Nos.)*		*1894–1917*			
Graduating			*1898–1900*	*1901–10*	*1911–20*	*Total*	*(Nos)*
INDEPENDENT	0.5	(1)	—	—	—	—	(—)
Clergy	6.5	(13)	14.3	9.4	6.8	8.1	(44)
Law	2.0	(3)	4.8	1.0	0.6	0.9	(5)
Medicine	1.5	(4)	—	2.0	1.9	1.8	(10)
Education*	7.5	(15)	9.5	6.9	9.9	8.8	(48)
Civil service†	5.0	(10)	—	2.0	9.9	1.5	(8)
Other professional	1.5	(3)	—	4.4	1.2	4.6	(25)
TOTAL PROFESSIONS	24.0	(49)	28.6	25.6	25.4	25.6	(140)
COMMERCE‡	13.6	(27)	14.3	15.8	10.6	12.6	(69)
INDUSTRY‡	1.5	(3)	—	2.5	2.8	2.6	(14)
FARMERS	16.1	(32)	19.0	20.7	19.6	20.0	(109)
CLERKS/TRADESMEN§	12.1	(24)	9.5	15.8	16.5	15.7	(87)
Skilled working class	12.6	(25)	9.5	11.3	14.0	12.8	(70)
Unskilled working class#	3.5	(7)	—	4.4	7.1	5.9	(32)
TOTAL W CLASS	16.1	(32)	9.5	15.8	21.1	18.7	(102)
NOT KNOWN**	16.1	(32)	19.0	3.9	4.0	4.6	(25)
Total %	100		100	100	100	100	
Numbers in sample		(199)	(21)	(203)	(322)	(546)	

See notes for table 6, p 79.
All students graduating before 1901 are included in the sample.

Trust. Five years later three-quarters of the female students were still obtaining Carnegie support ranging from £8. 18*s*. 1*d*. for arts to £19. 13*s*. 3*d*. for medicine.[9]

The average value of individual bursaries held by women increased only from £15. 10*s*. to £17. 10*s*. between 1895 and 1920.[10] Nor were women eligible for most of the presentation or 'modern' bursaries. Nevertheless the number of women holding arts bursaries ranging in value from £8 to £30 a year increased from seven in 1895 to twenty in 1920 and the total value of these bursaries, held for four years, increased from £436 to £1,416, almost all held by girls from state-supported schools.

Finally, from 1895 the SED paid bursaries of £20 for female Queen's/King's Students (men received £5 more) aiming specifically at a teaching career. The first three female Queen's Students were admitted to

Aberdeen in 1897 and by 1903–4 there were thirty-nine women students.[11] In 1902 the local committee which supervised Queen's/King's Students argued that as most of them came from families which could provide little or no financial assistance, the students should be permitted to hold both university and SED bursaries to enable them to attend the compulsory summer classes. At the time the SED paid the summer fees of almost all the students, but the winter fees of less than a half. SED bursaries were normally provided for two years, but the local committees were permitted to provide them for three, which enabled some of the students to graduate.[12]

Access to university education depended not only on the cost, but on the local availability of schooling which was both cheap and provided education up to university entrance level. By 1893 Scottish education was free for children up to the age of fifteen and the school boards in the North East encouraged secondary level work in any school rather than concentrating it in a few, with the result that one-third of the elementary schools receiving state aid in Banff and one-fifth of the schools in Aberdeenshire and Moray were presenting pupils for the university matriculation-level Leaving Certificate in 1900.[13] The twenty-eight female students admitted to Aberdeen in 1902 who went on to graduate had obtained all or part of their post-primary education in twenty-two or more different schools. At least two-thirds had attended a local elementary public school and over half were known to have received all their education at such a school.[14]

TABLE 9 SCHOOL EDUCATION OF ABERDEEN WOMEN GRADUATES MATRICULATING 1902.

County/Burgh	*No. of schools*	*% of students*	*School type*	*No. of schools*	*% of students*
Aberdeen City	4	35.7	Elementary*	18	58.9
Aberdeenshire	8	25.0	Grant-aided		
Banff	4	8.9	secondary	3	23.2
Moray	1	3.6	Private		
Ross	1	3.6	secondary	1	7.1
Orkney	3	10.7	Not known	?	10.7
Edinburgh	1	1.8			
Not known	?	10.7			
Total		100			99.9
Total number	22	28		22	28

*12 of these schools were subsequently designated higher grade public schools. Two of them were fee-paying.

Occupations of Aberdeen women graduates

Most of the Aberdeen University women graduates went into teaching—there were few other professional openings available to them except medicine, which appealed only to a minority while the more expensive training required meant it could be afforded only by middle-class students. Of the 4,539 students who graduated between 1901 and 1925, 67.8 per cent of women and 27 per cent of men went into education and 11 per cent of women and 42 per cent of men went into medicine.[15] Only a handful of women went into other occupations such as secretarial work, industrial research, the civil service, journalism or librarianship.

TABLE 10 ABERDEEN WOMEN GRADUATES (1898–1910): CAREER OR MARRIAGE BY FATHER'S OCCUPATION (PERCENTAGES).

	F.E.	*Teaching*	*Medicine*	*Other*	*Total paid work*	*No. occ./ married*	*No. in sample*
Clergy	6.8	50.0	22.8	6.8	86.4	13.6	(22)
Law	16.7	50.0	—	—	66.7	33.3	(3)
Medicine	—	50.0	25.0	—	75.0	25.0	(4)
Education	6.3	56.1	6.3	6.3	75.0	25.0	(14)
Civil Service	—	75.0	—	—	75.0	25.0	(4)
Other	11.1	38.9	11.1	16.7	77.8	22.2*	(9)
TOTAL PROF.	6.9	51.7	13.8	6.9	79.3	20.7*	(58)
COMMERCE	3.8	56.7	5.2	2.9	68.6	31.4*	(35)
INDUSTRY	—	60.0	—	20.0	80.0	20.0	(5)
FARMERS	6.5	67.4	5.4	3.3	82.6	17.4	(46)
TRADESMEN	6.4	83.3	—	1.5	94.1†	5.9*	(34)
Skilled	8.0	72.0	—	—	80.0	20.0	(25)
Unskilled	—	100.0	—	—	100.0	—	(9)
WORKING CLASS	5.9	79.4	—	—	85.3	14.7	(34)
NOT KNOWN	—	33.3	16.7	—	58.3†	41.7	(12)
Total %	5.8	63.4	6.3	4.0	80.4	19.6	
Numbers in sample	(13)	(142)	(14)	(9)	(180)‡	(44)	(224)

* Includes one died shortly after graduation.
† Includes one occupation unknown.
‡ Includes two occupations unknown.
Women with two careers counted as two halves; with three careers as three thirds (total rounded).

TABLE II Aberdeen women graduates (1911–1920): career or marriage by father's occupation (percentages).

	F.E.	*Teaching*	*Medicine*	*Other*	*Total paid work*	*No. occ./ married*	*No. in sample*
Clergy	19.6	24.4	22.7	15.1	81.8	18.2	(22)
Law	—	—	—	—	—	100.0	(2)
Medicine	—	50.0	50.0	—	100.0	—	(6)
Education	7.8	50.0	15.6	7.8	81.2	18.8	(32)
Civil Service	—	50.0	—	—	50.0	50.0	(4)
Other	2.1	51.9	12.6	8.4	75.0	25.0	(16)
TOTAL PROF.	8.8	42.3	18.3	8.6	78.0	22.0	(82)
COMMERCE	—	50.0	23.5	3.0	76.5	23.5	(34)
INDUSTRY	—	33.3	—	11.1	44.4	55.6	(9)
FARMERS	—	74.6	4.7	3.2	82.5	17.5	(63)
TRADESMEN	—	74.6	7.5	0.9	84.9*	15.1	(53)
Skilled working class	—	84.4	2.3	—	86.7	13.3	(45)
Unskilled working class	—	76.8	4.4	5.8	87.0	13.0†	(23)
TOTAL W CLASS	—	81.8	2.9	2.1	86.8	13.2†	(68)
NOT KNOWN	7.7	69.2	—	7.7	84.6	15.4	(13)
Total %	2.5	64	9.9	4.3	81.1	18.9	
Nos.	(8)	(206)	(32)	(14)	(261)*	(61)†	(322)

* One woman occupation unknown.
† Includes one woman who died shortly after graduating.
Graduates whose only paid employment was war-work have been excluded from the 'paid work' category.
Women with two careers counted as two halves; with three careers as three thirds (totals rounded).

The fact that most women entered the teaching profession does not end analysis of their occupational mobility. The profession in itself consisted of an accepted, if unsystematised, hierarchy of posts in terms of status and financial reward, and given that many of the Aberdeen women graduates who went into the education sector would have entered the teaching profession anyway, more detailed analysis of social origins and teaching careers is required to indicate whether a university education provided any new occupational opportunities (in addition to the more intangible cultural and academic influences). Much of the teacher training formerly provided by the denominational colleges was now provided in connection with the university; students receiving SED bursaries could only complete their teaching commitment at elementary (public or higher grade public) schools, and regulations had been introduced requiring teachers in grant-aided secondary schools to be honours graduates which required an additional year of expense many poorer students could not afford. The 'postgraduate' course established at St George's Training College, Edinburgh, for women intending to teach in secondary schools required a year's residence in Edinburgh and cost £20 for tuition alone and was therefore much too expensive for any but upper-middle-class girls.[16] Thus it was possible that university admission did not increase occupational opportunities for those women who went into teaching, but merely processed them and passed them into the educational system in the same stratified form as before.

TABLE 12 CAREERS OF ABERDEEN WOMEN GRADUATING 1898–1920 WHO WENT INTO SCHOOL TEACHING, BY FATHER'S OCCUPATION (PERCENTAGES).

	1898–1910				*1911–1920*			
	Elem.	*Sec.*	*Other*	*(Nos)*	*Elem.*	*Sec.*	*Other*	*(Nos)*
Professional	34.9	51.7	13.4	(30)	34.7	63.8	1.4	(35)
Commercial & Industrial	13.4	75.3	11.2	(22)	20.0	75.0	5.0	(20)
Farming	51.3	45.4	3.2	(31)	38.3	61.7	—	(47)
Tradesmen	19.4	78.8	1.8	(28)	31.7	63.4	5.1	(39)
Skilled W Class	43.6	52.0	4.5	(18)	32.9	64.5	2.6	(38)
Unskilled W Class	33.3	61.1	5.5	(9)	30.2	65.4	4.5	(18)
Not known	100.0	—	—	(4)	44.4	55.6	—	(9)
Total	34.7	58.6	6.7	(142)	33.2	64.3	2.5	(206)

'Elementary' includes primary and higher grade schools.
'Other' includes private or proprietary schools (mainly English) and foreign schools. Numbers rounded.

As table 12 shows, there were considerable variations in the recruitment of elementary and secondary teachers from the different social categories, but the form this took might not always be anticipated. Women from middle-class commercial and manufacturing families were least likely to teach in elementary schools and women from farming backgrounds were least likely to go into secondary education. More surprisingly, the highest proportion of secondary-level women teachers came from lower-middle-class backgrounds and the daughters of labourers were more likely to teach in secondary schools than women from professional families, though this statistic may be misleading as more than half of the earlier cohort of teachers from professional families taught in the higher grade public schools, many of which were providing education up to the same level as the designated secondary schools. The figures for the women who graduated between 1911 and 1920 show a far more even recruitment with approximately one-third teaching in elementary schools and two-thirds in secondary schools for all occupational categories except the daughters of commercial and industrial managers and owners, who remained far less likely to teach in primary schools. Middle-class women were more likely to move directly into secondary teaching posts whilst working-class and lower middle-class women generally taught in primary and higher grade schools first; women from these social backgrounds needed an SED bursary to enable them to obtain training and the period for which they were covenanted depended on the financial aid received.

The difficulty of obtaining a promoted post in a secondary school (only 6.7 per cent and 9.4 per cent of the two cohorts did so) reflected the difficulties women faced in gaining a foothold in the male-dominated Scottish co-educational system.[17] This was reinforced by women's own beliefs about their status and intellectual abilities, learnt from their home, school and university environment. The rector of Montrose Academy commented of an Aberdeen graduate who had attended his school as a pupil and then taught there for many years:

> She was content all her life to be an assistant teacher, being needlessly diffident about her own abilities, and having a curiously Victorian point of view regarding man's place in the universe—and in a department.[18]

Since the majority of Scottish schools were within the public sector, many women were also affected by the marriage bar which was widely applied and which prevented them from holding positions long enough to gain seniority. Thus of more than a thousand women graduating between 1901 and 1925 who were employed as school teachers, 42 per cent had retired on marriage by 1935.[19] Given the particular obstacles facing women seeking promotion in Scottish schools, it was perhaps surprising that only thirty-six of the women in the sample found employment at some point in English secondary schools. One constraint may have been the broadly-based Scottish general degree, taken by most of the arts students, which was unique to Scotland and left women facing competition from English graduates, most of whom held honours degrees.[20]

Almost one in every five of the 1898–1910 women graduates did spend some period of their life abroad, however, either working there or, more often, marrying men who worked or lived abroad, but this figure dropped to 5.6 per cent for the later cohort. Some 21 per cent of women graduating between 1898 and 1910 and 19 per cent of those graduating during the next nine years had no paid employment (or only war work), occasionally due to ill health, but most often because they married immediately after graduating.[21] By 1935, 45 per cent of the women graduating between 1898 and 1910, and 43.5 per cent of those graduating between 1911 and 1920 had married.

Upward social mobility

Being at university did not often result in socially-upward marriages; the nearest approximation was when a shepherd's daughter married a rural schoolmaster's graduate son. Often both partners came from non-professional backgrounds, as in the case of the daughter of a coachman from Kinmundy who married the son of a Turriff watchmaker who subsequently became vice-chancellor of the University of Bombay. However, many of the women graduates married local non-graduates; the graduate daughter of a signalman married a draper and the daughter of an Orkney labourer, who was employed after graduating as mathematics lecturer at the City of Leeds Training College, married a Lerwick fishcurer. Women from upper middle-class families were more inclined to marry men with similar backgrounds to themselves.

A point noted even by believers in the democratic tradition of Scottish education and its exemplification in the 'lad of parts', was the extent to which the educational facilities available were taken advantage of by individual families, rather than equally by all living in a locality. The Church of Scotland minister at Fyvie was 'fanatical' about education and willing to give up anything in order to get his nine children well educated: one daughter qualified in medicine at Edinburgh a year after Sophia Jex-Blake, two graduated at Aberdeen and a fourth took a domestic science and then a nursing course. The son of an Aberdeenshire village tailor noted that he was the only pupil in his class to go on to university; though there were others more talented, they were prevented by poverty and lack of parental interest. But in the tailor's family two sons and a daughter graduated (the daughter in medicine) and another daughter qualified as a teacher.[22]

Despite general support for an educational democracy which provided opportunity for upward social mobility for a competitive minority, the social class distinction between the lady of leisure and the working woman inevitably meant there was some doubt as to whether opportunities for upward social mobility for girls was an equally good thing. Christina Struthers was all too aware of existing prejudice in 1883 when she quoted the situation of women teachers as a reason for opening the Scottish universities to women:

> It must be clearly recognised, in pleading for the admission of women to the Scottish Universities, that it is desired, and can be fairly asked, not in the interest of any one class, but of the whole community. There is a disposition, on the part of some, to wish only such partial concession as shall consist with the maintenance of a certain social exclusiveness in our higher education of women; and to such the arguments drawn from the conditions applying to women teachers, under the national school system, seem uncalled for, as, it is maintained that the position they occupy, and the remuneration they receive, are, in reality, already beyond what the majority of them would command in any other walk, and above that of the social rank from which they come.[23]

Maria Ogilvie Gordon also wanted an 'opportunity for each individual woman—no matter in what status she is born',[24] but Mrs Harrower, who represented the more conservative element, commented wistfully, a few years after women's admission, that there had been a levelling down as well as a levelling up: 'At first the women who took part in the movement were the picked specimens, the choice spirits, but now . . . the most commonplace girl can study Hebrew or mathematics'.[25]

Analysis of fifty-four women who obtained research scholarships or were appointed to posts at Aberdeen University and therefore might be considered amongst the academic elite within the university (table 6) shows that opportunities for further advancement were biased in favour of upper middle-class students who constituted 41 per cent of those graduating but 58 per cent of the academic elite. At the other end of the social spectrum, there were no women from the lower working-class, and only 7.4 per cent of the group were from the upper working-class. Six of the women had no other paid employment; three were appointed to posts in scientific research institutes (one in Nigeria) and six became doctors, one of whom also lectured at a further education college. Of the eighteen who went into teaching, all but one taught at secondary schools, and ten spent some time teaching in England (one was senior classical mistress at the Girls' High School, Bedford; another taught English at Cheltenham Ladies College before being appointed lecturer at Somerville). Two become school inspectors, one a factory inspector and two became senior civil servants. Seventeen went into further education, twelve of them obtaining university posts in the women's colleges at Oxford, Cambridge and London, and at Birkbeck College and Birmingham and Cornell Universities. Doris Mackinnon, a lawyer's daughter, became the only professor, holding the chair of zoology at King's College, London.

Overall, however, Aberdeen women graduates did not have high-flying careers; only eight of the 226 women featured in a Scottish biography published in 1938[26] had attended Aberdeen University, and although this may have reflected the peripheral position of the university as viewed by Scottish 'society' as much as the quality of its graduates, the majority of Aberdeen women students were the daughters of rural professionals, farmers, merchants, tradesmen or skilled manual workers; and almost all of them moved into assistant teaching posts in state-aided Scottish schools.

20 After graduation – What? For lady students only. 'After graduation – what' was the title of a series of career articles published in *AM* between 1904 and 1909. Only one career (teaching) was recommended for women. *AM*, 26 (1908–9), p 17.

Conclusion

Nineteenth-century presbyterian Scotland was a patriarchal society but one in which women's personal responsibility for their spirituality was emphasised, a dichotomy which led to debate over women's position in the 1843 Church Disruption and their right to vote in church presbyteries. Whilst many presbyterians emphasised biblical teaching which supported women's subordinate role and rejected their need for access to any advice beyond that of the male members of the family, the close connection seen as existing between education and religion led others to argue that women ought to be well educated because self-improvement was a religious and moral duty, and therefore also a right. At the same time a more conservatively-rooted perception of the need for an educated understanding of contemporary religious controversies and increasingly sophisticated domestic responsibilities also developed.

By the third quarter of the century more Aberdonians were paying lip service to women's right to education, knowledge and truth, and even to the training necessary to enable women to earn an income in the medical or teaching profession if financial disaster should strike their family. However, few felt strongly enough to do anything positive to force through the changes in existing educational provision, social etiquette or class distinctions which were a necessary prelude to equality of educational opportunity for women. Opposition to higher education for women was less often made explicit since it could be expressed simply by maintaining the *status quo*. Humour or satire—still a powerful way of expressing social opinions which would otherwise be considered impolite—was a particularly important means of criticising women for the etiquette-conscious Victorian and Edwardian middle classes, and was used by the opposition both in pre-admission debates and later in the student magazine. Critics were anxious about professional competition, and considered that women were intellectually and physically inferior and that their activities should be restricted to a domestic and supportive role. In a small community such as Aberdeen the intellectual leaders were influential in this debate; many of the university professors were involved in public activities in which they had opportunities to express their opinion on the question of women's education.

At an institutional level, Aberdeen University lost out in the early years as a result of its failure to establish pre-admission provision for women. Lack of funds was a handicap, but as the example of St Andrews showed, this could have been overcome by more positive action. Crucial early decisions or, more accurately, procrastinations, included the lack of positive support for the 1874 and 1875 bills, the vote against admitting women in 1876 and the refusal to grant a title for the higher certificate. Aberdeen's small student-base and the conservative response of local middle-class women created difficulties which the university's own attitude did nothing to overcome. What was provided was too little, too late, enabling the other Scottish universities to gain the advantage. Yet, if Aberdeen University was no pioneer of higher education for women, at least a minority of Aberdeen's professors and other local supporters felt keenly enough about the issue to act as the opportunity arose, and to transfer to Aberdeen schools and university the gains made for women elsewhere in Scotland. As we have seen, by 1895 Aberdeen was the only Scottish university to have admitted women to both degrees and instruction in all its faculties.

Despite nineteenth-century English beliefs which Scottish propaganda often encouraged, Scottish education was very far from being comprehensively co-educational; nevertheless positive support for the principle of co-education was often evident. Lack of funds and the absence of outside support of a kind obtained in one form or another by almost every other British university were largely responsible for the want of facilities for female students at Aberdeen once they were admitted, but the democratic co-educational tradition was responsible for a surprising lack of institutional concern about the absence of such provision which was considered a necessity for female students elsewhere. At Aberdeen the university's existing facilities were seen as there to be taken advantage of by women if they wished—this was considered only fair, and followed the tradition of equality of opportunity for those male meritocrats who had succeeded in overcoming social and economic inequalities to reach the university; but apart from the half-hearted Castleton House residential scheme, no positive steps were taken to feminise the institution. No special teaching was arranged; no special bursaries were set aside; no special regulations were issued; no lady superintendent, matron or even ladies' committee was appointed to supervise and support the women students as a body.

Aberdeen lacked the social cachet of the other Scottish universities; its spartan provision and reputation as a 'poor man's university' made it especially difficult to attract upper and upper middle-class women students. Pollution boundaries, to use Delamont's terminology,[1] were also more rigidly enforced between upper middle-class men and women than between those in the lower middle class or working classes and the physical and social barriers between men and women were relatively informal at Aberdeen, though there was sometimes uncertainty as to whether a particular student activity was gender-related. Pressure on women students to adopt the existing student ethos led parents who were looking for a more feminine atmosphere to send their daughters to one of the women's colleges,[2] or at least to a university with protected and supervised residential accommodation for women students under the control of a lady warden or lady superintendent who could ensure female etiquette was maintained amongst the women, provide a strong guiding hand for young women entering university at a critical time of life when 'temptation' was at its strongest,[3] and make representations to the university authorities if she felt either staff or male students were transgressing the mores controlling relations between the sexes. The failure to appoint a permanent lady superintendent, or establish either residential accommodation or a union for women students at Aberdeen meant that the university had no senior woman, either academic or administrative, who could represent the interests of the female students and act as a role model, nor any physical centre around which women could develop an alternative culture to that of the male university.

Whilst the wealthier upper classes tended to stay away from Aberdeen and go instead to colleges where boundaries between men and women were more sharply drawn, women who did go to Aberdeen largely accepted the student ethos and it was some of the male students who tried to raise more distinctive barriers between the sexes. Those who objected to the presence of women or to the changing ethos of social life at the university recalled a halcyon past and criticised the women for destroying the old manly ethos and making the male students effeminate.[4] Portrayals of the future envisaging some form of role-reversal were one means of expressing anxiety under the cover of humour.[5] These also indicated the root of the male students' anxiety—power. This was reflected in anxiety about the relative numbers of male and female students.[6] Women could be tolerated so long as their ethos or culture was in the minority, at a level the university/class/society could assimilate; large numbers of women were problematic because they would change the nature of university life. Thus the increase of women in the arts faculty 'endangered the vote of the men so much' and the Literary Society was 'infested with women'.[7] Yet the male students who wrote such comments would be politeness itself at a personal level. Their dichotomous behaviour was based on an assumption of male superiority which as Bulloch had perceptively noted, resulted in 'gallantry' being used as a means of asserting men's pre-eminence. The debate about women's suffrage and the fight over the numbers which would ensure control of the SRC were more open, and the anxieties raised when the women began demanding power rather than accepting what they were given was reflected by increasingly strong criticism of their behaviour by the male students. The First World War led to a more assertive attitude amongst the women students, as the brief period when they became the student majority provided them with a space and a power base from which they could afford to be self-critical and self-confident.

Parental expectations and an increasing emphasis on domestic economy in elementary schools meant poorer girls faced greater difficulties than their male counterparts in obtaining higher education. But although the nineteenth-century 'lad of parts' has been shown to be as much myth as reality, nevertheless, a combination of Scottish and specifically local factors did mean that many lower middle-class and working-class girls were able to attend and graduate from Aberdeen University between 1894 and 1920. By the early twentieth century female students had taken over the symbiotic relationship between local schools and the university previously characteristic of male students from the North East. The war-time optimism about women doctors did not prove justified however; lacking encouragement student numbers declined fast, while those who qualified encountered difficulties in finding employment.[8]

Because 1860 to 1920 was the period when Aberdeen University's involvement in the education of women developed most rapidly concentration on this period alone increases the danger of an over-whiggish interpretation. Until the 1860s the idea of a university education for women was only dreamt of by eccentrics; in the 1870s and 1880s the possibility and then the means were debated; and in the 1890s women were admitted to the university. Thereafter there was a rapid increase in the number and proportion of female students and in the First World War they formed the majority. In the first decade of the twentieth century women arts students achieved a higher proportion of honours than men and by the end of the war women had moved into all faculties except divinity.

But as the pages of *Alma Mater* illustrated, many of the older attitudes lingered on after women's admission; in Delamont's terminology the women were a 'muted group'. Their peripheral position was reflected both formally and informally; formally, in their exclusion from certain bursaries and scholarships, in the absence of honorary degrees for women, in the small number and lowly status of female university staff and in women graduates not being permitted to vote for the university MP; and informally in incidents such as women students' constitutional minority on the SRC, women having 'no title' to existing student societies,[9] women graduates not being permitted to use the seats reserved for graduates[10] and regression over the Union—originally intended for

21 Stella the Bajanella. *AM*, 39 (1921–2), p 219.

both sexes but designed with men in mind, which by 1918 could be referred to as the 'men's union' without contradiction.[11] After the war women gained proportional representation on the SRC and a woman was appointed SRC president—but the circumstances were unique and it was to be another sixty-eight years before this occurred again. Even the numerical advance in women's share of higher education stopped; women were swamped by the post-war intake of male students, and although the proportion of women had increased again to 40 per cent by 1927, it had declined to 27 per cent nine years later, and even in 1987–8 women constituted only 43 per cent of the student total.

The first century of women's formal participation in university education at Aberdeen thus contains a mixture of advances and setbacks. The period 1860 to 1920 certainly saw some significant changes in old-established attitudes, opening the way for a substantial participation by women in university education. A feature of this process particular to Aberdeen was that—for a complex of reasons including institutional and personal poverty—women were admitted largely, if not completely, on the same terms as men. The half-serious, half-mocking year names the women were given—bajanellas and semilinas—neatly encapsulated their status.

Notes

Note: The abbreviation *AJ* has been used throughout for the *Aberdeen Journal*, although it was also known as the *Aberdeen Daily Journal*. Similarly, the abbreviation *AFP* has been used throughout for the *Aberdeen Free Press*, which at various times was titled *Aberdeen Daily Free Press* or *Daily Free Press*.

PREFACE (pp. xi to xii)

1 H Corr, 'The Schoolgirls' curriculum and the ideology of the home, 1870–1914', Glasgow Women's Studies Group, *Uncharted Lives: Extracts from Scottish Women's Experiences, 1850–1982* (Glasgow, 1983), 74–97; L Moore, 'Educating for the woman's sphere: domestic training versus intellectual discipline', E Breitenbach and E Gordon, eds, *Spheres of Struggle—the Public and Private Lives of Women in Scotland* (Edinburgh, forthcoming); L Moore, 'Invisible scholars: girls learning Latin and mathematics in the elementary public schools of Scotland before 1872', *History of Education*, 13 (1984), 121–37.

2 A welcome exception is R D Anderson, *Education and Opportunity in Victorian Scotland: Schools and Universities* (Oxford, 1983).

3 For a short account of Edinburgh University see S Hamilton, 'The First generations of university women 1869–1930', G Donaldson, ed., *Four Centuries of Edinburgh University Life 1583–1983* (Edinburgh, 1983), 99–115. For a fuller account see Sheila Hamilton's PhD thesis, 'Women and the Scottish Universities circa 1869–1939: a Social History' (University of Edinburgh, 1987).

CHAPTER 1 (pp. 1 to 11)

1 L G Anderson, *Elizabeth Garrett Anderson 1836–1917* (London, 1939), 108–9.

2 *Transactions of the National Association for the Promotion of Social Sciences [TNAPSS]*, Edinburgh meeting 1863, 361.

3 *AJ*, 18 June 1862.

4 K Burton, *Memoir of Mrs Crudelius* (Edinburgh, 1879).

5 D Masson, *University Teaching for Women: Lecture Introductory to the English Literature Course* (Edinburgh, 1868). Other Aberdeen graduates who helped the movement for the higher education of women included

Alexander Bain (Bedford); Robert Alexander Neil (Girton and Newnham); George Macdonald (Bedford); Andrew Findlater (Bedford); John Gray McKendrick (Edinburgh and Glasgow) and George Croom Robertson (University College, London).

6 'University education for women in Scotland', *The Ladies' Edinburgh Magazine [LEM]*, 5 (November 1879), 517; 'The Rise of the higher education of women movement in Glasgow' in *The Book of the Jubilee in Commemoration of the Ninth Jubilee of the University of Glasgow 1451–1901* (Glasgow, 1901), 126–38.

7 E.g. Professor Gray and his successor gave public lectures on natural philosophy from 1854 to 1860 under the auspices of the Mechanics' Institute and from 1854 to 1864 professor's assistant, Mr (from 1861, Professor) Brazier lectured on chemistry to men and women.

8 *AJ*, 28 October 1868; *AFP*, 3 November 1868.

9 L Moore, 'Aberdeen and the higher education of women 1868–1877', *Aberdeen University Review [AUR]*, 48, (1980), 280–303, esp. 288–91.

10 S Jex-Blake, *Medical Women: a Thesis and a History* (Edinburgh, 2nd ed., 1886; Facsimile reprint Source Books Press, 1970).

11 *Hansard's Parliamentary Debates*, CCXIX, 37 Vict., 1526–60 and CCXXII, 38 Vict., 1123–70.

12 Moore, 'Higher education of women', 289–91.

13 *Scotsman*, 27 April 1874. Dickie retired in 1877 and Bain in 1880.

14 *AFP*, 16 June 1874, 5 March 1875; *AJ*, 10 March 1875; *Aberdeen Herald*, 6 March 1875.

15 *AJ*, 12 May 1875.

16 *AFP*, 9 April 1877; Aberdeen University Library [AUL], MS U 370/1, University of Aberdeen, Senatus Minutes [Senatus Minutes], 7 April 1877.

17 Forbes's half-sister was reputed to have attended the public, but university approved, chemistry classes taught by her father, the professor of humanity at King's College, in the 1830s.

18 M Hay, 'The Rev. James Smith, minister of Newhills', *AUR*, 5, (1917–18), 134.

19 Moore, 'Higher education of women', 296–8.

20 L R Moore, 'The Aberdeen Ladies' Educational Association, 1877–1883', *Northern Scotland*, 3 (1979–80), 123–57.

21 Mrs Bain, Mrs Geddes, Mrs Milligan and Mrs Struthers.

22 Those who lectured to the association included Professors J Black, F Fuller, W D Geddes, J S Brazier, J Struthers, W Milligan, W M Minto, J C Ewart, H A Nicholson, J Donaldson, J H Trail, S D F Salmond (UF Church College) and J Harrower (then a professor's assistant).

23 Aberdeen Public Library [APL], MS Lo376 Ab3, Aberdeen Ladies' Educational Association Minutes [ALEA Minutes], 29 March 1882; Aberdeen Ladies' Educational Association [ALEA], *Fifth Annual Report*, (1882) (a set of the published annual reports is pasted into the minute book); *AFP*, 1 April 1882.

24 W Milligan, *The Higher Education of Women; being a Lecture Delivered by*

Professor Milligan of the University of Aberdeen in Opening the Ladies' Classes at Aberdeen, for Session 1877–78, (Aberdeen, 1877; reprinted from *AFP*, 3 November 1877).

25 *AFP*, 2 November 1878. An attempt to establish a governess register in Aberdeen failed.

26 Associations in larger cities such as Glasgow, Edinburgh and Manchester encountered similar problems.

27 ALEA, *Fifth Annual Report* (1882).

28 *AFP*, 27 October 1881; 27 October 1882.

29 Professor Pirie, quoted *AFP*, 27 October 1881; ALEA Minutes, 9 February 1883; *AJ*, 7 September 1885.

30 Editorial, *AJ*, 2 May 1883; C Struthers, *The Admission of Women to the Scottish Universities* (Aberdeen, 1883; a revised and extended version of an article in *AFP*, 24 March 1883), 16–17; *AFP*, 24 August 1872. For other criticisms see *AFP*, 9 January 1874.

31 ALEA, *Sixth Annual Report* (1883).

CHAPTER 2 (pp. 12 to 19)

1 Letters, *AJ*, 21 and 22 August 1882; A Bain, *Autobiography* (London, 1904), 304; see also *AJ*, 14 October 1863. But it was suggested at an Aberdeen, Banff and Moray Schoolmasters' Association meeting that the university should start examinations for girls as well as boys (*AJ*, 8 January 1868).

2 Moore, 'Ladies' Educational Association', 133–4.

3 Ibid., 135–7.

4 Letter from J Struthers, *AJ*, 21 August 1882.

5 *AFP*, 15 September 1890.

6 *AJ*, 28 August 1880, quoted in Moore, 'Ladies' Educational Association', 138.

7 APL, MS Lo376, ALEA Minutes, 5 and 11 March 1878; 29 October 1878.

8 Ibid., 5 March 1880.

9 Ibid., 23 April 1880; AUL, MS U 370/2, Senatus Minutes, 3 May and 5 August 1880, 5 March 1881; AUL, MS U 202, Aberdeen University Local Examination Minutes [AULE Minutes], 26 February and 22 April 1881.

10 ALEA, *Memorandum on the Institution of a Title or Degree of L.A. in Connection with the Proposed Higher Certificate for Women* (1881) (a copy is pasted in the ALEA Minute Book); ALEA, *Fourth Annual Report* (1881), 7–8.

11 Throughout this work 'public' school is used in the Scottish sense of an elementary school under a local educational authority.

12 W Knight, *A History of the L.L.A. Examination and Diploma for Women, and of the University Hall for Women Students at the University of St Andrews*

(Dundee, 1896). Figures for 1888–1904 were given annually in *St Andrews University Calendar.*

13 *Memorandum on the Institution of a Title*, 3; A Mackie, 'The Higher Certificate for Women', *Educational News*, 11 (13 and 20 November 1886), 803–4, 820–1. Higher Certificate results were issued in Aberdeen University's annual *Local Examinations Calendar.*

14 Moore, 'Ladies' Educational Association', 143–4. Women who held the LLA were generally paid at graduate level up to 1905, R N Smart, 'Literate ladies—a fifty year experiment', *St Andrews University Alumnus Chronicle*, 59 (June 1968), 21–31.

15 Moore, 'Ladies' Educational Association', 142–3.

16 ALEA, *Fifth Annual Report* (1882).

17 E.g. Trail (*AJ*, 13 September 1886); Christie and Milligan (*AJ*, 12 September 1887); Niven (*AJ*, 16 September 1889).

18 *AJ*, 7 September 1885.

19 *AJ*, 15 September 1884; John Black also supported it in his last public speech (*AJ*, 29 August 1881).

20 *AJ*, 12 September 1887; 7 September 1885; *AFP*, 15 September 1890.

21 *AJ*, 16 September 1889, 13 September 1886.

22 Mackie, 'The Higher Certificate for Women'.

23 A reference to Dr David Rennet, mathematics tutor.

24 A Mackie, W C Spence, A M Williams, *To the Senatus of the University of Aberdeen* (loose sheet with AUL Special Collections copy of Struthers' *Admission of Women*).

25 AUL, MS U 370/2, Senatus Minutes, 1 and 29 October 1887.

26 AUL, MS U 202, AULE Minutes, 29 February 1888.

CHAPTER 3 (pp. 20 to 36)

1 J Burstyn, *Victorian Education and the Ideal of Womanhood* (London, 1980). The importance of male educational superiority for the maintenance of patriarchy was spelt out in the editorial, *AJ*, 17 November 1869 and see also *AFP*, 8 September 1868.

2 C Struthers, *The Admission of Women to the Scottish Universities*, 4.

3 Burstyn, *Victorian Education.*

4 AUL, MS 597, Aberdeen Philosophical Society Minute Book, 3 November 1848 and 2 February 1849; [J D Milne], *Industrial and Social Position of Women in the Middle and Lower Ranks* (London, 1857). A revised and updated edition incorporating 1861 census data was published in 1870 under the title *Industrial Employment of Women in the Middle and Lower Ranks.* Milne, a graduate of Marischal College, was an important mid-nineteenth-century feminist. He corresponded with J S Mill and was quoted by the *Englishwoman's Journal* and Harriet Martineau.

5 E C Brown, *The Kildrummy Christies* (Aberdeen, 1948), 68.

6 E.g. *AFP*, 9 and 27 July 1869; 22 June 1870; 23 April and 15 August 1874; 5 March 1875; Professor Struthers (*AJ*, 7 September 1885).
7 *AFP*, 16 July 1869; AUL, MS U 282, Aberdeen University Debating Society [Debating Society] Minutes, 10 January 1890.
8 E.g. 'Profitable employment of women lady physicians', *Milne's Register of Facts and Occurrences relating to Literature, the Sciences, and the Arts*, 4 (November 1860), 34–5; *Aberdeen Water-Cure Journal and Family Guide to Health*, 2 (February 1860), 39 and (September 1860), 198; Moore, 'Higher education', 287–8; *AFP*, 1 July 1876; *Alma Mater* [*AM*], 5 (1887–8), 129.
9 See, for example, John Black's views in *Report of the Committee of Council on Education 1865–66* [*RCCE*] (HMSO), 291; L Lumsden, 'Woman's work; girls' schools', *LEM*, 1 (1875), 208–20 and 238–46, esp. 219–20; L I Lumsden, *On the Higher Education of Women in Great Britain and Ireland* (Aberdeen, [1884]), 11. In 1887 Principal Geddes referred to certain local schools as having 'descended to a female teacher' (M Cruickshank, *History of the Training of Teachers in Scotland* (London, 1970), 87). For examples of the attitudes of local teachers and parents see letters in *AFP*, 19 November 1875, 25 October 1879 and 18 September 1882.
10 I Chalmers, 'A University training and degree for women', paper read to Aberdeen EIS (*AFP*, 10 October 1881); *AFP*, 23 April 1874.
11 Ibid. See also *AFP*, 9 February 1875. A similar view expressed by HMI William Jolly was quoted in *AFP*, 8 June 1874.
12 *AFP*, 6 April 1876.
13 Moore, 'Ladies' Educational Association', 149–50; *AFP*, 11 May and 6 January 1883. See also *AM*, 9 (1890–91), 164.
14 Scottish Universities Commission [SUC], *General Report of the Commissioners under the Universities (Scotland) Act, 1889* (Edinburgh, HMSO, 1900), 297; 'Correspondence between the Scotch Education Department and the Aberdeen University . . . with reference to the training of teachers at the Universities of Aberdeen and St. Andrews', *RCCE* (1885), 95–102. Cruickshank (114) says Aberdeen proposed organising a male teacher training department.
15 AUL, MS U 202, AULE Minutes, 3 September 1889; ALEA, *Fourth Annual Report* (1881); AUL, MS U 370/1, Senatus Minutes, 15 December 1877; ALEA, *Fifth Annual Report* (1882).
16 Informal interview, 7 July 1981.
17 'University education of women in Scotland', *LEM*, 5 (1877), 517.
18 E.g. *Bon Accord*, 2 (5 February 1887); 3 (16 April 1887), 15; 3 (9 July 1887), 9; 3 (13 August 1887), 16.
19 *Castle Sceptre*, 10 (25 July 1877), 35–6.
20 Ibid., 80 (1 May 1883), 348.
21 Ibid., 125 (1 February 1887), 528.
22 [A Black], 'The L.L.A. Degree', *Aberdeen High School Magazine*, 1 (1) (March 1885), 16.
23 AUL, MS U 281, Debating Society Minutes, 26 November 1886, and

see also *The Academic*, 5 (1877–8), 96; *AM*, 2 (1884–5), 116; *AM*, 10 (1892–3), 38.
24 *AM*, 4 (1886–7), 25.
25 Ibid., 134.
26 [Black], 'The L.L.A. Degree'.
27 *AM*, 11 (1893–4), 79.
28 *Report of Women's Conference on Women's Work, held in the Music Hall Buildings, Aberdeen, on 9th, 10th and 11th October, 1888* (Aberdeen, 1888), 75–6.
29 *AM*, 4 (1886–7), 32; see also *AFP*, 16 June 1874.
30 *AJ*, 28 August 1880.
31 Struthers, *The Admission of Women*, 3.
32 Burstyn, *Victorian Education*, 139.
33 E.g. *AJ*, 28 October 1868 and *AFP*, 12 March 1869 quoted in Moore, 'Higher education', 281 and 288; *AFP*, 2 April 1869; 2 December 1876; Milligan, quoted *AFP*, 12 September 1892.
34 Milligan, *Higher Education*.
35 *AJ*, 28 August 1880.
36 Milligan, *Higher Education*.
37 A graphic account of domestic chores in the Milligan household appears in Katherine Trail, *Reminiscences of Old Aberdeen* (Aberdeen, 1932).
38 E.g. *AJ*, 10 November 1873; *AFP*, 23 April 1874.
39 Struthers, *The Admission of Women*, 12–13.
40 Milligan, *Higher Education*.
41 W D Simpson, ed., *The Fusion of 1860. A Record of the Centenary Celebrations and a History of the United University of Aberdeen 1860–1960* (Edinburgh, 1964), 140; W Robertson Nicol in *Alma Mater Quarter-Centenary Number* (1906).
42 Mrs Henry Sidgwick, *Health Statistics of Women Students of Cambridge and of Oxford and their Sisters* (Cambridge, 1890).
43 J D Milne, *On the Secondary Education of Girls* (Aberdeen, 1877); ALEA, *Fourth Annual Report*; Mackie, Spence and Williams, *To the Senatus of the University of Aberdeen*.
44 *AFP*, 28 August 1883.
45 *AJ*, 7 September 1885.
46 *AJ*, 21 August 1882.
47 *AFP*, 6 January 1883.
48 *AFP*, 14 September 1891.
49 *AFP*, 27 October 1881; 16 April 1883.
50 E.g. *AM*, 2 (1884–5), 116; 11 (1893–4), 79; 17 (1899–1900), 113; 21 (1903–4), 72; 34 (1916–17), 112; AUL, MS U 282, Debating Society Minutes, 10 January 1893.
51 Milligan, *Higher Education*; *AFP*, 27 August 1883.
52 *AFP*, 9 August 1887.
53 *AJ*, 16 September 1889.
54 J Harrower, *Introductory Address to Senior Greek Class 1888–9* (Aberdeen, 1888).

55 R S Rait, *The Universities Commission 1889–1897; a Review* (reprinted from the *Banffshire Journal*, 11 January 1898), 22.
56 The University of London admitted women to degrees in 1878 and to full membership in 1880; Bristol College admitted women in 1876; Victoria University in 1880 (but the first college, Owen's College, Manchester, in 1883); the Welsh colleges in 1884.
57 *Report of Women's Conference on Women's Work*, 75.
58 *AFP*, 15 September 1890.
59 Anderson, *Education and Opportunity*, 70–102.
60 J Struthers had made the same point (*AFP*, 12 June 1877).
61 A Mackie, 'The Higher Certificate for Women', *Educational News*, 11 (13 and 20 November 1886), 804. John and Christina Struthers and J Duguid Milne were all critical of the existing MA syllabus and in 1881 Isabella Chalmers recommended an alternative equivalent three-year degree for male and female teachers, omitting Latin and Greek and incorporating French and German, physical and natural science, physiology and the laws of health.
62 Struthers, *The Admission of Women*, 13.
63 Scottish Record Office [SRO], ED/26/9, *Statement by the Senatus of the University of Aberdeen regarding Extension of the University Buildings*, 21 October 1886.
64 *AFP*, 31 October 1883.
65 *AFP*, 15 September 1890; *AJ*, 7 September 1885.
66 *AFP*, 12 September 1892.

CHAPTER 4 (pp. 37 to 53)

1 University of Aberdeen, *Minutes of the General Council*, 7 June 1890.
2 SRO, MS ED/9/41, letter from James W H Trail to the SUC, 1 July 1891.
3 AUL, MS U 370/3, Senatus Minutes, 6 February 1892.
4 SRO, MS ED/9/128/2211, letter from Aberdeen University SRC to the SUC.
5 *AJ*, 15 June 1892.
6 AUL, MS U 301/2, Aberdeen University Students' Representative Council [SRC] Minutes, 21 May 1892.
7 *AM*, 10 (1892–3), 3.
8 AUL, MS U 370/3, Senatus Minutes, 4 June 1892; 11 June 1892; *AJ*, 13 June 1892. Anderson postponed his motion until the Senatus report was received.
9 AUL, MS U 370/3, Senatus Minutes, 2 July 1892.
10 *AJ*, 13 July 1892.
11 Scottish Universities Commission, *General Report . . . 1889*, minutes of 14 and 26 October 1891.
12 *AJ*, 13 July 1892.
13 AUL, MS U 370/3, Senatus Minutes, 2 and 26 July 1892.

14 Ibid., 25 February 1896.
15 Ibid., 25 May 1896; N Shepherd, 'Women in the university; fifty years 1892–1942', *AUR*, 29, (1941–2), 176. The student, Myra McKenzie, was nicknamed 'granny' because she was considerably older than most of the other medical undergraduates.
16 See, for example, the debate over the admission of women students to Edinburgh Royal Infirmary and the Western Hospital, Glasgow.
17 Committee on Scottish Universities [CSU], *Minutes of Evidence taken before the Committee on Scottish Universities, with Index* (HMSO, 1910) (Cd. 5258) para. 224–6.
18 Informal interview, 15 December 1975; *AM*, 31 (1913–14), 275.
19 CSU, *Report of the Committee on Scottish Universities, with Appendix* (HMSO, 1910) (Cd. 5257), 9; and *Minutes*, para. 224.
20 University of Aberdeen, *Minutes of the Aberdeen University Court*, 4, 13 November 1894.
21 *AM*, 10 (1892–3), 27; *Aberdeen University Arts class, 1893–97. Class record, 26th December, 1913* (Aberdeen, 1913).
22 M P Ramsay, 'Women students in Aberdeen University', *The World of Dress and Woman's Journal*, November 1906; *AM*, 26 (1908–9), 225.
23 The course was subsequently increased to one year.
24 Aberdeen Provincial Committee for the Training of Teachers, *Minutes of Meeting*, 2, 24 December 1908; CSU, *Minutes*, para. 234.
25 Informal interview, 15 December 1975.
26 CSU, *Minutes*, para. 232–4 and Appendix VI, p. 44; Provincial Committee, *Minutes*. Later the committee held some of the courses at its training centre.
27 SRO, MS ED/7/2/7 copy of letter from Mr J Struthers to Mr Sellar dated 19 March 1908; *AM*, 26 (1908–9), 83–4.
28 Calculated from University of Aberdeen, *Report as to Statistics under the Universities (Scotland) Act, 1889.*
29 Calculated from T Watt, *Roll of Graduates of the University of Aberdeen 1901–1925 with Supplement 1860–1900* (Aberdeen, 1935), Appendix B.
30 D I Mackay, *Geographical Mobility and the Brain Drain: a Case Study of Aberdeen University Graduates 1860–1960* (London, 1960), 78.
31 Personal communication.
32 Calculated from T Watt, *Roll of Graduates.*
33 Royal Commission on the Civil Service, *Second Appendix to the Fourth Report of the Commissioners* (HMSO, 1914) (cd. 7340), 22.
34 The Carnegie Trust for the Universities of Scotland, *Annual Report*, (1901–). The grants awarded to (Dame) Maria Ogilvie Gordon, D Sc, for geological research have been counted amongst those awarded to Aberdeen women. She was the daughter of Dr A Ogilvie (head of Robert Gordon's College) and lived in Aberdeen, but was actually a graduate of University College London and the first woman there to receive a D Sc.
35 University Ordinance no. 58, General, no. 2.

36 *AFP*, 24 September 1894; *AM*, 12 (1894–5), 8. According to Anderson the suggestion came from Professor Trail, Library Curator (*AUR*, 6 (1918–19), 41).
37 *AM*, 29 (1911–12), 85; N Shepherd, 'Elizabeth Christie Brown', *AUR*, 37, 242–4; E C Brown, *The Kildrummy Christies*, 75–6. She was technically appointed only for a trial session, but held the post for thirty years.
38 *AM*, 21 (1903–4), 17; M P Ramsay, 'Women students in Aberdeen University'.
39 CSU, *Minutes*, para. 230.
40 Calculated from the *Aberdeen University Calendar*.
41 Informal interview, 15 December 1975; *AUR*, 44 (1971–2), 107–8.
42 *AM*, 13 (1895–6), 184.
43 Shepherd, 'Women in the University', 176.

CHAPTER 5 (pp. 54 to 65)

1 AUL, MS U 370/3, Senatus Minutes, 3 February 1894.
2 SRO, MS ED/9/109(4282), Memorial to the Scottish Universities Commission by the Students' Representative Council of Aberdeen anent Draft Ordinances – General, nos. XIX and XX.
3 SRO, MS ED/9/109(4179), Memorial by the General Council of the University of Aberdeen to the Scottish Universities Commission on Draft Ordinance, General, no. 19 and General, no. 20, dated 5 April 1894; *Minutes of the General Council*, 1, 11 April 1894.
4 CSU, op. cit., *General Report*, xxix.
5 *Senatus Minutes*, 1, 30 March 1895.
6 *Minutes of the Aberdeen University Court*, 4, 14 May 1895.
7 This was successfully opposed.
8 J Lillie, *Tradition and Environment in a Time of Change* (Aberdeen, 1970), 9.
9 *Senatus Minutes*, 1, 30 March 1895.
10 AUL, MSS U 15-U 39, University of Aberdeen Bursary Competitions (1894–1920).
11 E.g. *AM*, 13 (1895–6), 8; 17 (1899–1900), 184; 20 (1902–3), 185.
12 Ibid., *Aberdeen University Calendar*.
13 *AM*, 12 (1894–5), 35, 55; 14 (1896–7), 3.
14 *AM*, 15 (1897–8), 189.
15 *AM*, 18 (1900–1), 175; 19 (1901–2), 185.
16 SUC, op. cit., pp. xxix–xxx and minutes, 7 May 1891.
17 Ibid., pp. xxiix and xxxi.
18 *AJ*, 8 September 1884.
19 I M Caesar [née Asher], 'A Bajanella of 1894', *AUR*, 29 (1941–2), 182.
20 D G M'Lean, ed., *The History of Fordyce Academy: Life at a Banffshire School 1592–1935* (Banff, 1936), 142.
21 Ibid., 134–5, 141.
22 *AM*, 15 (1897–8), 186.

23 *AM*, 17 (1899–1900), 175; 16 (1898–9), 195–6; 18 (1900–1), 175–6; 22 (1904–5), 181.
24 *AM*, 16 (1898–9), 195–6.
25 Ibid., *Minutes of the Aberdeen University Court*, 5, 20 February 1900.
26 Ibid., *AM*, 16 (1898–9), 195–6.
27 The point was urged more strongly by educationalists than those in commerce (Anderson, *Education and Opportunity*, 279).
28 *AM*, 18 (1900–1), 175.
29 *AM*, 16 (1898–9), 195–6.
30 *Minutes of the Aberdeen University Court*, 5, 20 February, 13 March 1900.
31 Ibid., 13 May 1902.
32 Ibid., 10 June 1902.
33 In 1922 three out of forty-two presentation foundations were open to women.

CHAPTER 6 (pp. 66 to 86)

1 *Senatus Minutes*, 1, 11 January 1896.
2 Ibid., 30 April 1896.
3 *AM*, 14 (1896–7), 222–3; 15 (1897–8), 199.
4 R McWilliams-Tullberg, *Women at Cambridge: a Men's University – Though of Mixed Type* (London, 1975), 42–9, 57–9, 99–100.
5 Anderson, *Education and Opportunity*, 328–30; Carnegie Trust, *Tenth Annual Report* (1910–11), 4; University Grants Committee [UGC], *Second Report of the University Grants Committee* (HMSO, 1921), 14; R M Pinkerton, 'Of chambers and communities: student residence at the University of Edinburgh, 1583–1983', G Donaldson, ed., *Four Centuries of Edinburgh University Life, 1583–1983* (Edinburgh, 1983). 116–30.
6 *AM*, 15 (1897–8), 173; 14 (1896–7), 222–3.
7 *Minutes of the General Council*, 1, 15 April 1896; *AM*, 15 (1897–8), 199; *Aberdeen University Calendar 1899–1900*, Appendix B; JML, 'Girl student life in Aberdeen', *The Lady* (8 January 1903), 45; E W Watt, 'A Bajan of 1894', *AUR*, 29 (1941–2), 186; *AM*, 16 (1898–9), 53.
8 JML, 'Girl student life in Aberdeen'. Residential accommodation was not popular with student teachers either.
9 Aberdeen Local Committee, *Memorandum as to the Bearing of the Carnegie Trust on the University Training of Teachers* (Aberdeen, [*c*1903]); informal interview, 15 December 1975.
10 Informal interview, 16 February 1976; Ramsay, 'Women students in Aberdeen University'.
11 J H Lobban, 'King's College—1888–1895', *Alma Mater Quarter-Centenary Number* (1906), 46; *AM*, 32 (1914–15), 141.
12 AUL, MS U 842/6, University of Aberdeen, Finance Committee Minutes, 30 January and 13 February 1911. For subsequent approaches, J Scotland, '"T.C.": a History of Aberdeen College of Education', *Education in the North*, 6, Supplement, p. vii.

13 'Proposed Elphinstone Hall', *AUR*, 5 (1917–18), 58–69, 161–4; 'Residence for students', ibid., 261–4; Anderson, *Student Community at Aberdeen*, 88.
14 UGC, *Returns from Universities . . . 1919–20.* King's College and the LSE did not offer accommodation. Aberdeen still provided no residential accommodation for female students in 1941.
15 A F B Roberts, 'Student life and work, 1910', *Education in the North*, 6 (1969), 14.
16 Ibid., 15; Scotland, '"T.C."', p. xiii.
17 Provincial Committee, *Minutes*, 2, 20 September 1907.
18 *AM*, 19 (1901–2), 42; 21 (1903–4), 193; the Welsh attitude was partly the result of earlier problems.
19 Informal interview, 15 December 1975.
20 McWilliams-Tullberg, *Women at Cambridge*, 59, 103, 144, 169–70; P Griffin, ed., *St Hugh's: One Hundred Years of Women's Education* (Basingstoke, 1986), 31; M Vicinus, *Independent Women: Work and Community for Single Women, 1850–1920* (London, 1985), 134, 146–7; informal interview, 16 February 1976.
21 McWilliams-Tullberg, *Women at Cambridge*, 70; Griffin, *St Hugh's*, 30; Shepherd, 'Women in the University', 174–5; informal interview, 26 February 1976. Chaperones were required at dances, *AM*, 31 (1913–14), 250, 261.
22 Informal interview, 15 December 1975; *AM*, 35 (1917–18), 14; 31 (1913–14), 225 (quotation).
23 Informal interview, 10 February 1977; *AM*, 28 (1910–11), 68.
24 *AM*, 15 (1897–8), 41.
25 *AM*, 22 (1904–5), 71.
26 *AM*, 34 (1916–17), 53.
27 Ibid., 80.
28 Informal interview, 15 December 1975.
29 *AM*, 19 (1901–2), 159.
30 The women were provided with two rooms and could get tea and buns from the steward. The SRC attempted to get the women students to contribute towards the cost but the university authorities agreed to donate £2 a year.
31 *AM*, 28 (1910–11), 167 (quotation); 29 (1911–12), 177; 34 (1916–17), 88.
32 *AUR*, 8 (1920–1), 257.
33 *AUR*, 9 (1922–3), 259; 10 (1923–4), 75, 168; Anderson, *Student Community*, 94.
34 *AM*, 26 (1908–9), 223–5.
35 *AM*, 31 (1913–14), 151.
36 *AM*, 15 (1897–8), 38; 25 (1907–8), 69; 34 (1916–17), 49–50.
37 Based on sample from Watt, *Roll of Graduates*.
38 Anderson, *Student Community*, 136.
39 Ramsay, 'Women students in Aberdeen University'.
40 C Dyhouse, *Girls Growing up in Late Victorian and Edwardian England* (London, 1981); *AM*, 24 (1906–7), 44.

41 *AM*, 30 (1912–13), 114; 35 (1917–18), 40.
42 *AM*, 21 (1903–4), 83.
43 Informal interview, 16 February 1976.
44 M G Clarke, *A Short Life of Ninety Years* (London, 1973), 16–17.
45 *AM*, 21 (1903–4), 154.
46 *AM*, 28 (1910–11), 103.
47 Ramsay, 'Women Students in Aberdeen University'.
48 I.e. SRC/*Alma Mater*/student club/society committee members or giving papers at meetings.
49 Vicinus, *Independent Women*, 140.
50 Based on a sample from Watt, *Roll of Graduates*. Occupational categories assigned follow Anderson, *Education and Opportunity*, 308 fn.
51 Analysis of Oxford women found death of the father had no significant influence on post-university experience (J Howarth and M Curthoys, 'The Political economy of women's higher education in late nineteenth- and early twentieth-century Britain', *Historical Research*, 60 (142), June 1987, 208–31).
52 Lillie, *Tradition and Environment*, 33.
53 *AM*, 13 (1895–6), 53; 24 (1906–7), 171.
54 *AM*, 18 (1900–1), 26, 28; 22 (1904–5), 38.
55 Watt, 'A Bajan of 1894', 185.
56 *AM*, 21 (1903–4), 78, 89, 169 (quotation).
57 Ibid., 162.
58 R Annand Taylor, 'The Coming of the women students', *Alma Mater Quarter-Centenary Number* (1906), 55–7; *AM*, 26 (1908–9), 80; 23 (1905–6), 11.
59 *AM*, 17 (1899–1900), 11, 27, 37.
60 *AM*, 21 (1903–4), 57, 68, 163; 22 (1904–5), 16–17, 19, 26 (quotation), 40; Lillie, *Tradition and Environment*, 33 (quotation).
61 *AM*, 22 (1904–5), 162.
62 Annand-Taylor, 'The Coming of the women students', 56.
63 AUL, MSS, U 281–2, Debating Society Minutes, 21 October 1898. (An impromptu debate on the subject was held in 1910.)
64 Ramsay, 'Women students in Aberdeen University'.
65 S Hamilton, 'The First generations of university women 1869–1930', G Donaldson, ed., *Four Centuries of Edinburgh University Life 1583–1983*, 108–9.

CHAPTER 7 (pp. 87 to 103)

1 *AM*, 12 (1894–5), 41.
2 *AM*, 15 (1897–8), 21, 31; 16 (1898–9), 36.
3 *AM*, 18 (1900–1), 75; 20 (1902–3), 86.
4 *AM*, 22 (1904–5), 162 (quotations), 179.
5 AUL, MS U 301/3, SRC Minutes, 17 February 1906.
6 *AM*, 24 (1906–7), 29.

7 Ibid., 31, 38.
8 Ibid., 41.
9 Ibid., 131.
10 Ibid., 131, 132, 154.
11 AUL, MS U 301/3, SRC Minutes, Report of the election committee, 26 January 1907; 9 February 1907.
12 *AM*, 24 (1906–7), 171.
13 Ibid., 152.
14 *AM*, 25 (1907–8), 49.
15 *AM*, 24 (1906–7), 173; 30 (1912–13), 235.
16 *AM*, 24 (1906–7), 131.
17 *AM*, 25 (1907–8), 197.
18 AUL, MS U 301/3, SRC Minutes, undated meeting after 12 December 1908.
19 Ibid., 26 February 1910, 18 February and 17 June 1911.
20 AUL, MS U 301/5, SRC Minutes, 18 November 1922.
21 Informal interview, 15 December 1975.
22 AUL, MS U 281, Debating Society Minutes, 11 December 1868.
23 *AM*, 2 (1884–5), 116; 11 (1893–4), 132; 17 (1899–1900), 113; AUL, MS U 282, Debating Society Minutes, 12 January 1900.
24 *AM*, 18 (1900–1), 4.
25 *AM*, 23 (1905–6), 91, 214.
26 *Minutes of Aberdeen University Court*, 6, 22 February 1906.
27 L Moore, 'The Women's suffrage campaign in the 1907 Aberdeen by-election', *Northern Scotland*, 5 (2) (May 1983), 155–78; *AM*, 24 (1906–7), 167, 172.
28 *AM*, 25 (1907–8), 195, 206, 219.
29 Ibid., 228.
30 *AJ*, 18 May 1908.
31 *AM*, 26 (1908–9), 68.
32 *AM*, 14 (1896–7), 46; 17 (1899–1900), 53. The first female candidates for the rectorship stood in 1939.
33 *AJ*, 5, 20 and 26 June 1908.
34 *AM*, 26 (1908–9), 8.
35 *The Suffragette*, 1 (28 October 1908); *The Carsonian*, 5 (30 October 1908), 14.
36 *AM*, 26 (1908–9), 25. The meeting was chaired by Edith Morrison, who became a close friend of suffragette Emily Davison (L Stanley and A Morley, *The Life and Death of Emily Wilding Davison* (London, 1988), 134–46).
37 *AM*, 26 (1908–9), 42.
38 Informal interview, 26 February 1976. Manchester University did threaten Chrystabel Pankhurst with expulsion.
39 Anderson, *Student Community*, 80; *AM*, 26 (1908–9), 50, 54. At a meeting of over 50 Liberal women students at the beginning of the campaign, 43 supported Asquith (*AJ*, 26 June 1908).
40 *AM*, 26 (1908–9), 37, 68, 87, 125, 132.

41 *AM*, 30 (1912–13), 114, 201; informal interviews, 26 February 1976; 10 February 1977.
42 *AM*, 30 (1912–13), 178; informal interview, 26 February 1976.
43 *AM*, 27 (1909–10), 123; 29 (1911–12), 143, 238.
44 *AM*, 31 (1913–14), 201; Anderson, *Student Community*, 30, 70.
45 M G Clarke, *A Short Life of Ninety Years* (London, 1973).
46 The illustration is reproduced in M Mackenzie, *Shoulder to Shoulder: a Documentary* (Harmondsworth, 1975), 204. Helen Ogston explained her reason for carrying a whip in a letter to *Votes for Women*, 10 December 1908, 179.
47 Informal interviews, 15 December 1975, 16 February 1976. Fenton Wyness did not name Helen Ogston but did refer to the perpetrator as a 'well-known local campaigner', *City by the Grey North Sea: Aberdeen* (Aberdeen, 1965), 254.
48 *AJ*, 2, 3 and 6 December 1912; Stanley and Morley, *Emily Wilding Davis*, 159–60.
49 Informal interview, 26 February 1976. For examples of both views held by male graduates see *Aberdeen University Arts Class, 1890–4. A Record of Thirty Years* (Aberdeen, 1924), p. vii.
50 *AUR*, 3 (1915–16), 270.
51 *AM*, 34 (1916–17), 42.
52 Ibid., 40, 65 (quotation); informal interview, 16 February 1976.
53 *AM*, 32 (1914–15), 1; 33 (1915–16), 32, 52, 93; 34 (1916–17), 42.
54 AUL, MS U 282, Debating Society Minutes, 10 June and 29 October 1920.
55 *AM*, 35 (1917–18), 37–8; 32 (1914–15), 157 (quotation).
56 *AM*, 32 (1914–15), 193, 198; 33 (1915–16), 9.
57 *AM*, 32 (1914–15), 120, 154, 178; 34 (1916–17), 9, 108; 35 (1917–18), 10, 24.
58 *AM*, 35 (1917–18), 10.
59 Ibid., 13.
60 Ibid., 12.
61 Ibid., 49–50.

CHAPTER 8 (pp. 104 to 119)

1 I M Caesar [née Asher], 'A Bajanella of 1894', *AUR*, 29 (1941–2), 182. See also *AM*, 12 (1894–5), 197. 'Cinderellas' were university dances ending before midnight.
2 M P Ramsay, 'Women students in Aberdeen University', *The World of Dress and Woman's Journal*, November 1906.
3 *AM*, 21 (1903–4), 44.
4 AUL, MS U 282, Debating Society Minutes, 17 November 1911; AUL, MS U 301/3, SRC Minutes, 5 May 1909 (emphasis added).
5 E W Watt, 'A Bajan of 1894', *AUR*, 29 (1941–2), 185. See also *AM*, 35 (1917–18), 40.

6 *AM*, 14 (1896–7), 25, 35.
7 *AM*, 23 (1905–6), 35. Women students' hats were a frequent source of complaint at Cambridge, see R McWilliams-Tullberg, *Women at Cambridge: a Men's University—Though of Mixed Type* (London, 1975). There were many references, often humorous, to women students' hats at Aberdeen. See S Delamont, *Knowledgeable Women: Structuralism and the Reproduction of Elites* (London, 1989), chapter 4 for an analysis of the symbolic importance of clothing for female pupils and students.
8 Anderson, *Student Community*, 13, 47–8; *AM*, 22 (1894–95), 149, 170.
9 Annand-Taylor, 'The Coming of the women students', 56; *AM*, 14 (1896–7), 25.
10 AUL, MSS U 301/2–3. SRC Minutes, 21 June 1902, 17 October 1903.
11 Anderson, *Student Community*, 28–30, 37–40.
12 *AM*, 18 (1900–1), 81.
13 *AM*, 21 (1903–4), 42; AUL, MS U 301/3, SRC Minutes, 21 January 1910.
14 *AM*, 10 (1892–3), 16; 18 (1900–1), 16, 65.
15 L Hutton, *Literary Landmarks of the Scottish Universities* (New York, 1904), 133–4; *Journal des Débats*, quoted *AM*, 22 (1904–5), 192.
16 *AM*, 22 (1904–5), 92, 108 (quotation).
17 Ibid., 91, 104; 23 (1905–6), 82; 24 (1906–7), 71.
18 *AM*, 25 (1907–8), 115, 117 (quotation).
19 University of Aberdeen, *Arts Class 1908–1912. Class Record* (Aberdeen, 1954).
20 *AM*, 14 (1896–7), 46, 170; 21 (1903–4), 95; 22 (1904–5), 38, 162.
21 *AM*, 21 (1903–4), 166, 169; 25 (1907–8), 83; 29 (1911–12), 262, 276; 31 (1913–14), 38.
22 Anderson, *Student Community*.
23 Watt, 'A Bajan of 1894', 185.
24 See chapter 3, footnote 49.
25 E.g. *AM*, 13 (1895–6), 151; 17 (1899–1900), 70; 24 (1906–7), 131; 28 (1910–11), 213.
26 E.g. *AM*, 10 (1892–3), 54; 20 (1902–3), 1; 21 (1903–4), 99; 22 (1904–5), 145.
27 *AM*, 17 (1899–1900), 113; 20 (1902–3), 74; 22 (1904–5), 145; 24 (1906–7), 38; 25 (1907–8), 117.
28 *AM*, 21 (1903–4), 133.
29 *AM*, 23 (1905–6), 31.
30 *AM*, 24 (1906–7), 31.
31 Ibid., 154.
32 Ibid., 152.
33 *AM*, 29 (1911–12), 213–14.
34 W K Leask, 'A Notable class record', *AUR*, 1 (1913–14), 55–66; J M Bulloch, 'If I were a bajan again', ibid., 256.
35 *AM*, 12 (1894–5), 130; 19 (1901–2), 179; 26 (1908–9), 225; 29 (1911–12), 227–8.
36 *AUR*, 11 (1923–4), 124.

37 *AM*, 14 (1896–7), 195; 15 (1897–8), 5, 13, 14–15; 18 (1900–1), 18, 45.
38 *AM*, 18 (1900–1), 28.
39 Committee on Scottish Universities [CSU], *Minutes*, para. 227.
40 *AM*, 33 (1915–16), 105; 34 (1916–17), 108, 112; 35 (1917–18), 40.
41 *AM*, 31 (1913–14), 118.
42 *AM*, 34 (1916–17), 97.
43 Ibid., 112.
44 Ibid., 65–6.
45 *AM*, 29 (1911–12), 262; 31 (1913–14), 118; 34 (1916–17), 112.
46 *AM*, 29 (1911–12), 276; 31 (1913–14), 132, 151; 34 (1916–17), 112.
47 *AM*, 26 (1908–9), 197, 223–5; 27 (1909–10), 6.
48 *AM*, 29 (1911–12), 213–14.
49 Ibid., 262, 227–8.
50 CSU, *Report*, Appendix II, 30–1.
51 Anderson, *Student Community*, 40–1.
52 *AM*, 21 (1903–4), 169; 24 (1906–7), 152.
53 Watt, *Roll of Graduates*, appendix A and sample.
54 *AM*, 25 (1907–8), 93; informal interview, 15 February 1977.
55 *AM*, 29 (1911–12), 227–8.
56 *AM*, 10 (1892–3), 11.

CHAPTER 9 (pp. 120 to 132)

1 Anderson, *Student Community*, 135.
2 Informal interview, 15 February 1977.
3 AUL, MSS U 15–29, University of Aberdeen Arts Bursary Competition.
4 AUL, MS U 7, Students Register, Faculty of Arts.
5 *AM*, 22 (1904–5), 52.
6 Aberdeen Local Committee, *Memorandum*.
7 UGC, *Returns from Universities and University Colleges . . . 1919–20*.
8 The figures for women students are taken from Anderson, *Education and Opportunity*, 314–15.
9 Carnegie Trust for the Universities of Scotland, *Tenth Annual Report* (1910–11); *Fifteenth Annual Report* (1915–16).
10 Estimated from *Aberdeen University Calendar*.
11 SED, *Training Colleges. Reports for the Year 1899* (HMSO, 1900) (xxvi), 52; Anderson, *Student Community*, 58.
12 Aberdeen Local Committee, *Memorandum*.
13 Anderson, *Education and Opportunity*, 219–23.
14 University of Aberdeen, *Record of the Arts Class of 1902–1906* (Aberdeen, 1927).
15 Estimated from Watt, *Roll of Graduates*, Appendix A.
16 N Shepley, *Women of Independent Mind: St George's School, Edinburgh and the Campaign for Women's Education 1888–1988* (Edinburgh, 1988), 16–32.

17 M G Clarke, *A Short Life of Ninety Years* (London, 1973); L I Lumsden, *On the Higher Education of Women in Great Britain and Ireland* (Aberdeen, [1884]), 6, and 'Woman's work; girls' schools', *LEM*, 1 (1875), 219–20; H Corr, 'The Sexual division of labour in the Scottish teaching profession, 1872–1914', W M Humes and H Paterson, eds, *Scottish Culture and Scottish Education 1800–1980* (Edinburgh, 1983), 137–50.
18 University of Aberdeen, *Bajan's Jubilee. Record of the Arts Class 1901–1905* (Aberdeen, 1951).
19 Watt, *Roll of Graduates*, Appendix A.
20 MacKay, *Geographical Mobility and the Brain Drain*, 85.
21 If no occupation was given it was assumed there was none. Using the same data Mackay estimated that only 4.6% of women graduating 1901–21 had no paid employment, but he included war work and also recorded 7.2% 'occupation unknown'.
22 Informal interview, 15 February 1977; H Diack, *That Village on the Don* (Nottingham, 1965). See also *AM*, 22 (1904–5), 184; D G M'Lean, ed., *The History of Fordyce Academy: Life at a Banffshire School 1592–1935* (Banff, 1936), 97–8.
23 Struthers, *Admission of Women*, 9.
24 M Ogilvie Gordon, *On the Teaching of Girls* (Aberdeen, 1904), 7. See also Professor Patterson's comment reported *AFP*, 6 October 1902.
25 R Harrower, *Opening Addresses delivered to the Aberdeen University Women Students' Debating Society 1899 and 1903* (Aberdeen, privately printed [*c*1903]), 20.
26 *Scottish Biographies 1938* (London, 1938).

CONCLUSION (pp. 133 to 138)

1 S Delamont, *Knowledgeable Women: Structuralism and the Reproduction of Elites* (London, 1989).
2 E.g. M G Clarke, *A Short Life of Ninety Years* (London, 1973), 20.
3 *AM*, 29 (1911–12), 177.
4 *AM*, 18 (1900–1), 76; 20 (1902–3), 66; 21 (1903–4), 95; 24 (1906–7), 152; *Aberdeen University Arts Class, 1890–4*, p. vii.
5 *AM*, 16 (1898–9), 104; 24 (1906–7), 162.
6 *AM*, 23 (1905–6), 55; 24 (1906–7), 131, 154; 25 (1907–8), 49.
7 *AM*, 24 (1906–7), 154; 21 (1903–4), 162.
8 H Diack, *That Village on the Don* (Nottingham, 1965), 107; *AUR*, 12 (1924–5), 185.
9 *AM*, 21 (1903–4), 166.
10 Informal interview, 15 December 1975.
11 *AM*, 35 (1917–18), 40.

APPENDIX 1 ABERDEEN UNIVERSITY STUDENTS

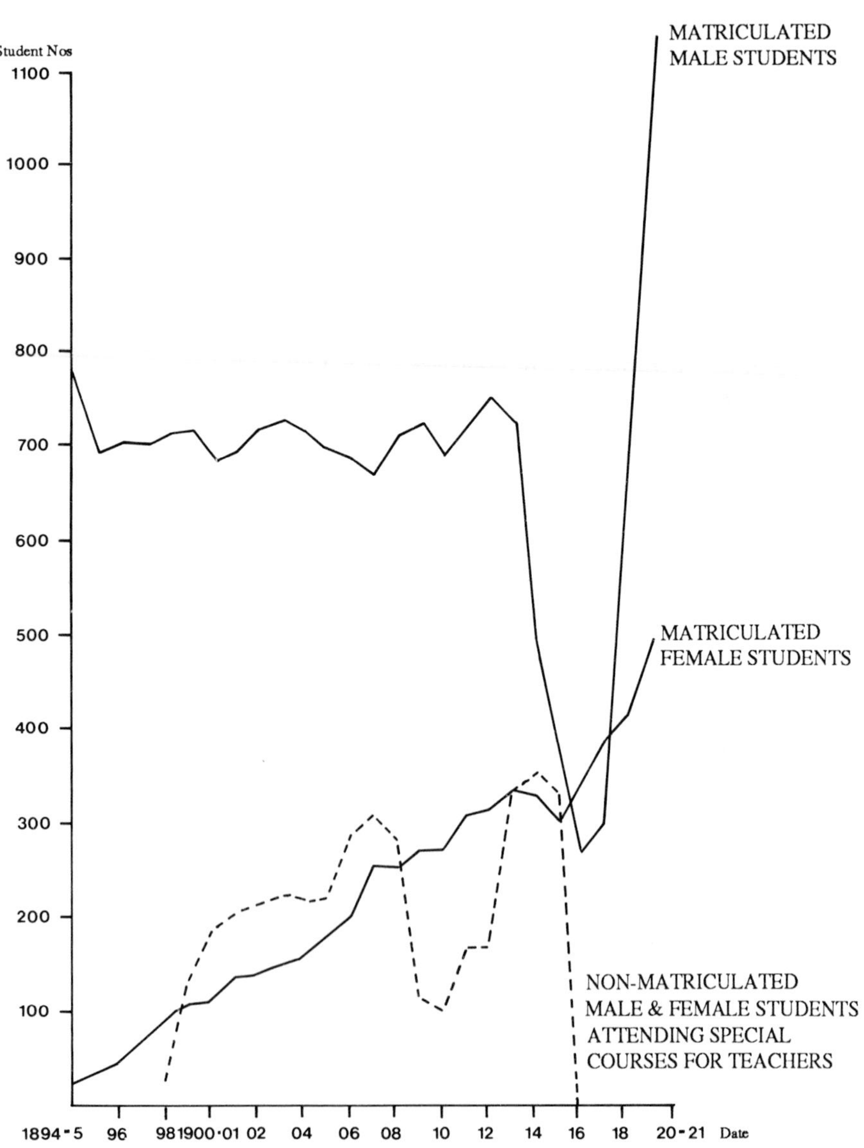

Bibliographical Note

There are few published primary or secondary sources on any aspect of the history of the higher education of women in Scotland. The majority of those that do exist relate to the campaign to obtain medical education for women, and most were published as pamphlets or articles. James Craigie's seminal *Bibliography of Scottish Education 1872–1972*, 245 pages in length, contains only twenty items on the higher education of women. Of these, only three primary sources are of particular relevance to Aberdeen. *Women in Scotland: an Annotated Bibliography*, published by the Open University in Scotland in 1988, adds another forty-six publications on higher education, of which only four secondary works relate to Aberdeen.

It is therefore not surprising that the history of the development of higher education for women at Aberdeen University relies largely upon fragmentary and fugitive sources. Information on the position of women at Aberdeen prior to their admission is largely dependent on reports in the local press and on the minutes and reports of the Aberdeen Ladies' Educational Association. References in the Court, Senatus or General Council minutes of Aberdeen University are tantalisingly few and even these initiatives often ran into the sand, apparently never to be taken up again.

The Aberdeen student newspaper *Alma Mater* is an invaluable source of information on student attitudes and activities from 1894. The graduate periodical, *Aberdeen University Review*, started in 1913, provides useful reminiscences and biographical information, while student class records from 1894 onwards also contain information about female members. In the Quincentennial Studies series, Robert Anderson's *Student Community at Aberdeen 1860–1939*, summarises the influences behind these sources and provides a graphic account of the student community, breaking new ground in its account of the impact of the admission of women students in 1892.

Accounts by women students themselves are more difficult to find. In addition to the few contemporary descriptions and reminiscences, information was obtained through informal interviews conducted by the author during the 1970s with Mrs Murray Smith, both a daughter and a granddaughter of Aberdeen professors, and with five women graduates who matriculated between 1907 and 1914: Dr Mary Esslemont, Dr Isabella Leitch, Mrs Mackenzie Stuart, Mrs Ramsay Ewan and Miss Nan Shepherd. Nan Shepherd had provided the only prior historical account of women at Aberdeen University, written to commemorate the fiftieth anniversary of their admission.

In addition this study owes much to a wide range of English writings on women's education and feminist issues, a convenient bibliography of which may be found in Sara Delamont's *Knowledgeable Women*. Scotland has still to produce any theoretical works which provide comparable insights on the history of women's education within its own borders.

Index